POLYGLOT

How I Learn Languages

POLYGLOT

How I Learn Languages

KATÓ LOMB

Translated from the
Hungarian by Ádám Szegi

Edited by Scott Alkire

TESL-EJ Publications
Berkeley, California & Kyoto, Japan

Thank you to Elizabeth Collison, Elena Smolinská,
Sylvia Rucker, Professor Thom Huebner, and Dr. Maggie Sokolik
for their help with this project.

The review comments of Dr. Larissa Chiriaeva, Maria Çomsa, MA, and
Dr. Stefan Frazier were invaluable in the preparation of the manuscript.

Translated by Ádám Szegi.
The first two Forewords, Introduction, and Chapter 20
were translated by Kornelia DeKorne.

Originally published in Hungary as *Így tanulok nyelveket* by AQUA
Kiadó, Budapest, in 1995 [1970]. Copyright © 1995 AQUA Kiadó.

Publisher's Cataloging-in-Publication Data
Lomb, Kató, 1909–2003.
Polyglot : how I learn languages / Kató Lomb. — 2nd English ed.
p. cm.
Library of Congress Control Number: 2008907032
ISBN 978-1-60643-706-3

1. Language learning. I. Title

Cover: *The Tower of Babel*
Pieter Bruegel the Elder (1563)

TESL-EJ Publications
Berkeley, California & Kyoto, Japan

10 9 8 7 6 5 4 3 2 1

Contents

≈

Preface

≈

IF multilingualism is indeed one of the "great achieve-ments of the human mind," as Vildomec (1963, p. 240) claims, it is regrettable that few linguists have studied poly-glots and what it is they know about language learning.[1] For their part, polyglots have not provided us with much information either; in the 20th century, texts by polyglots on language learning, in particular texts that relate how they actually learned their languages, are rare.

One text by a polyglot that relates personal language-learning experience is Dr. Kató Lomb's *Polyglot: How I Learn Languages* (2008; Hungarian: *Így tanulok nyelveket* [1995, 4th ed.]). A collection of anecdotes and reflections on language and language learning, it frequently recalls the pragmatism of similar texts by polyglot linguists such as Bloomfield,[2] Pei,[3] and Pimsleur.[4] Lomb's text, however, is distinguished by the fact that it is the product of a learner who acquired most of her languages as an adult, including several at native-like competency. And while it is not for-mally academic, Lomb's work is particularly worthy of study because several of her hypotheses about language learning correlate with the findings of SLA researchers in the past 25 years.

---

1. Linguistic definitions of multilingualism/polyglot vary. Nation, in a study of "good" language learners, defines a multilingual person as being fluent in four or more languages (1983, p. 1).
2. *Outline Guide for the Practical Study of Foreign Languages*, 1942.
3. *How to Learn Languages and What Languages to Learn*, 1973.
4. *How to Learn a Foreign Language*, 1980.

"The most multilingual woman"

Dr. Kató Lomb (1909–2003) has been called "possibly the most accomplished polyglot in the world" (Krashen, 1997, p. 15) and "the most multilingual woman" (Parkvall, 2006, p. 119). Unlike most polyglots, Lomb came to language learning relatively late. Indifferent to foreign languages in secondary school and university (her PhD was in chemistry), she began to acquire English on her own in 1933 to find work as a teacher. She began learning Russian in 1941, and by the end of World War II was interpreting and translating for the Budapest City Hall. She continued to learn languages, and at her peak was interpreting and/or translating 16 for state and business concerns. In the 1950s she became one of the first simultaneous interpreters in the world, and by the 1960s her reputation was such that, according to an interview in *Hetek* newspaper (14 November 1998), she and her colleagues in the Hungarian interpreting delegation were known as "the Lomb team" (p. 16).

Her accomplishments did not alter her essential modesty: "It is not possible [to know 16 languages]—at least not at the same level of ability," she wrote in the foreword to the first edition of *Így tanulok nyelveket* (1970). "I only have one mother tongue: Hungarian. Russian, English, French, and German live inside me simultaneously with Hungarian. I can switch between any of these languages with great ease, from one word to the next.

"Translating texts in Italian, Spanish, Japanese, Chinese, and Polish generally requires me to spend about half a day brushing up on my language skills and perusing the material to be translated.

"The other six languages [Bulgarian, Danish, Latin, Romanian, Czech, Ukrainian] I know only through translating literature and technical material."

Interest in Lomb's book remained steady in Hungary for several years; subsequent editions were published in 1972, 1990, and 1995. In addition, translations were published in

Japan, Latvia, and Russia. Lomb went on to write books on languages, interpreting, and polyglots, and continued learning languages into her eighties. In 1995 she was interviewed by Stephen Krashen, who brought her achievements to the attention of the West.

Form and content of Így tanulok nyelveket

Perhaps because Lomb believes that language and language learning are phenomena that can be understood in different ways, she employs different writing styles—memoir/narrative, functional/expository, and figurative/literary—to convey different aspects of language and language learning. She uses memoir/narrative to relate most of her language-learning experiences, functional/expository prose to outline her language-learning strategies, and figurative/literary passages to conceptualize language and language acquisition.

Lomb's functional/expository sections feature many strategies that correlate to the strategies of successful learners documented in major SLA studies (see Alkire, 2005); a few others do not, or have not yet been studied. One of her unique language-learning strategies is the reading of books at the beginning of language study. In Chapter 7 she writes, "Dare to include [extensive] reading in your learning program from the very beginning," and in Chapter 8 she asserts that the bulk of a learner's knowledge will come not from dictionaries, course books, or teachers, but from books. In autobiographical passages, Lomb relates her experiences learning English, Russian, and Spanish through novels. All of this is noteworthy because the reading of full-length texts (e.g., novels) to acquire languages has not been studied by SLA researchers.

Lomb is also singular in not endorsing grammar study. She writes, "The traditional way of learning a language (cramming 20–30 words a day and digesting the grammar supplied by a teacher or course book) may satisfy at most one's sense of duty, but it can hardly serve as a source of joy. Nor will it likely be successful." For emphasis Lomb paraphrases Toussaint and Langenscheidt, the 19th-century publishers: *"Man lernt Grammatik aus der Sprache, nicht Sprache aus der Grammatik."* (One learns grammar from language, not language from grammar.)

About textbooks Lomb takes an original and provocative stance. She writes, "A student whose native language is Hungarian should study from a book prepared by a Hungarian. This is not owing to chauvinism but because every nation has to cope with its own specific difficulties when learning a foreign language. Jespersen, the eminent Danish philologist, knew this: he classified the errors committed in English by nationality."

Although many of Lomb's principles have been corroborated by SLA research, the preceding points—the value of extensive reading at nascent learning stages, the backwardness of emphasizing grammar, and the benefits of learning from a textbook written by a compatriot—remain relatively unexplored, and are deserving of more SLA research.

How Lomb conceptualizes language learning is compelling and suggests that the imagination plays a greater role in language acquisition than is commonly understood. Lomb writes, "To use a metaphor, the Russian language is a complicated, massive cathedral harmoniously fashioned in every arch and corner. The learner must accept this in order to have sufficient motivation to 'build' it." Also: "Knowledge—like a nail—is made load-bearing by being driven in. If it's not driven deep enough, it will break when any weight is put upon it." Elsewhere Lomb opines, "A foreign language is a castle. It is advisable to besiege it from all directions: newspapers, radio, motion pictures which are not dubbed, technical or scientific papers, textbooks, and the visitor at your neighbor's."

Lomb employs other metaphors as well. To illustrate teacher-guided learning, she presents a wry Hungarian joke and then kindly explains the symbolism:

Coffees in Budapest have an advantage—
    they have no coffee substitute
They have a disadvantage—
    they have no coffee bean
And they have a mystery—
    what makes them black?

As Lomb explains it, "You can discover these elements in teacher-guided learning as well.

"Its unquestioned advantage: the reliability of the linguistic information and the regularity of the lessons. [School is what it says it is, for better or worse.]

"Its disadvantage: inconvenience, an often-slow pace, and less opportunity for selective learning. [School is often not conducive to real learning.]

"In the end, the classic, teacher-guided method has its own mystery." [What makes school "school"?]

Figurative language runs throughout Lomb's book and suggests, perhaps, that the imaginative conceptualization of language learning may in fact facilitate it.

Factors in language learning success

Throughout her book Lomb expresses her belief that a language learner's success is primarily determined by motivation, perseverance, and diligence—and not by innate ability. "I don't believe there is [an innate ability for learning languages]," she says. "I want to demystify language learning, and to remove the heroic status associated with learning another language." She claims that a good method "plays a much more important role in language learning than the vague concept of innate ability." She also believes that a learner's level of education may play a role in how successful he or she is in acquiring a language; she speculates that educated people may be *less* successful at learning languages because of the gap between their intellectual achievements and their status as beginning learners. Finally, Lomb states that "The ideal solution, of course, is to maintain active relationships with native speakers of one's ilk and interests, with lots of shared activities—especially if these natives are willing to correct your mistakes, and if one is resolved not to get mad at them when they do." One wonders if any "solution" to language learning has ever been stated so well.

Lomb recognizes that language learning is time-intensive and offers advice accordingly. We "should connect language learning with either work or leisure. And not at the expense of them but to supplement them." Also: "Spend time tinkering with the language every day. If time is short, try at least to produce a 10-minute monologue." These dictums may seem simple or obvious, but they are seldom incorporated in academic language-learning programs.

Languages, the only thing worth knowing even poorly

Despite her own high level of achievement, Lomb claims that she is not a perfectionist in language learning. "I like to say that we should study languages because languages are the only thing worth knowing even poorly," she writes.

"If someone knows how to play the violin only a little, he will find that the painful minutes he causes are not in proportion to the possible joy he gains from his playing. The amateur chemist spares himself ridicule only as long as he doesn't aspire for professional laurels. The man somewhat skilled in medicine will not go far, and if he tries to trade on his knowledge without certification, he will be locked up as a quack doctor.

"Solely in the world of languages is the amateur of value. Well-intentioned sentences full of mistakes can still build bridges between people. Asking in broken Italian which train we are supposed to board at the Venice railway station is far from useless. Indeed, it is better to do that than to remain uncertain and silent and end up back in Budapest rather than in Milan." Lomb never loses sight of the fact that language learning should be pragmatic.

Implications for SLA theory

Krashen and other linguists have offered arguments for why the experiences of Lomb and other successful learners are important to SLA theory.

1. "[Lomb] demonstrates, quite spectacularly, that high levels of second language proficiency can be attained by adults; much of her language acquisition was done in her 30s and 40s..." (Krashen and Kiss, 1996, p. 210). Stevick (1989), Chang (1990), Gethin and Gunnemark (1996), and Parkvall (2006) report other cases of outstanding adult learners. These cases are important exceptions to prevailing SLA theory on age and language learning and need to be accounted for.

2. Pavlenko argues that texts such as Lomb's allow for a "complex, theoretically and socio-historically informed, investigation of social contexts of language learning and of individual learners' trajectories, as well as an insight into which learners' stories are not yet being told" (2001, p. 213).

3. Krashen and Kiss point out that Lomb was a relatively unsuccessful student of languages in high school and learned them primarily later, through self-study (1996). The implications of this for prescribed methods in language teaching are worthy of investigation.

4. In an article on Lomb's strategies for language learning and SLA theory, Alkire notes that Lomb's text "has strategies for, and conclusions about, language learning that closely correlate with those of successful learners documented in major SLA studies of the past 25 years" (2005, p. 17).

5. Inspired by Carroll (1967), Naiman, Fröhlich, Stern, and Todesco conducted a study to see if "biographies of individuals speaking more than one language might

contain clues to the conditions of successful language acquisition" (1978, p. 1). Their findings substantiated their thesis and have been widely influential in SLA theory; Brumfit calls their work "still of great relevance" (1996, p. vii).

6. Scovel writes that, in our efforts to understand successful language learning, "The evidence can be either experimental or experiential. Given the complexity of SLA, I think we need a lot of both..." (2001, p. 10).

As stated at the outset, there are not many accounts of language learning by polyglots, nor are there many case studies of them. Yet such learners, by virtue of their accomplishments, must be accounted for in any meaningful theory of SLA. Stevick, in his study of successful learners, writes:

"[Successful learners'] statements are in fact data—not, to be sure, data about what they did, but data about what they said they did. And these data need to be accounted for.... As data, these statements sometimes fit in with various theories of second language learning, and sometimes challenge them. Whenever there is an apparent inconsistency between one of these statements and a given theory, then the theory must either show that the statement should not be taken seriously, or it must show how the statement is in fact consistent with it after all, or the theory must modify itself accordingly" (1989, pp. xii–xiii).

Dr. Lomb's text offers rare, experiential data that may well contribute to our understanding of SLA.

—Scott Alkire
San José State University
June 2008

References

Alkire, S. 2005. Kató Lomb's strategies for language learning and SLA theory. *The International Journal of Foreign Language Teaching*, Fall.

Brumfit, C. 1996. Introduction to the new edition. In Naiman et al., *The good language learner* (pp. vii–x). Clevedon: Multilingual Matters Ltd.

Chang, C. 1990. *How I learned English*. Taipei: Bookman Books Ltd.

Gethin, A. and Gunnemark, E. V. 1996. *The art and science of learning languages*. Oxford: Intellect.

Krashen, S. D. and Kiss, N. 1996. Notes on a polyglot. *System* 24 (2):207–210.

Krashen, S. D. 1997. *Foreign language education the easy way*. Culver City (CA): Language Education Associates.

Lomb, K. 1995. *Így tanulok nyelveket*. Budapest: AQUA Kiadó.

Naiman, N., Fröhlich, M., Stern, H. H., and Todesco, A. 1996. *The good language learner*. Clevedon: Multilingual Matters Ltd.

Nation, R. J. 1983. The good language learner: A comparison of learning strategies of monolinguals, bilinguals, and multilinguals. PhD diss. University of California, Santa Cruz.

Parkvall, M. 2006. *Limits of language*. London: Battlebridge.

Pavlenko, A. 2001. Language learning memoirs as a gendered genre. *Applied Linguistics* 22 (2):213–240.

Scovel, T. 2001. *Learning new languages*. Boston: Heinle & Heinle.

Stevick, E. W. 1989. *Success with foreign languages*. New York: Prentice Hall.

Vildomec, V. 1963. *Multilingualism*. Leydon, The Netherlands: A. W. Sythoff.

Foreword to the
First Edition

≈

IF IN conversation my knowledge of languages is revealed, people tend to ask the same three questions. In response, I give the same three answers.

Question: Is it possible to know 16 languages?

Answer: No, it is not possible—at least not at the same level of ability. I only have one mother tongue: Hungarian. Russian, English, French, and German live inside me simultaneously with Hungarian. I can switch between any of these languages with great ease, from one word to another.

Translating texts in Italian, Spanish, Japanese, Chinese, and Polish generally requires me to spend about half a day brushing up on my language skills and perusing the material to be translated.

The other six languages [Bulgarian, Danish, Latin, Romanian, Czech, Ukrainian] I know only through translating literature and technical material.

Question: Why haven't you chosen a career in foreign language teaching?

Answer: In order to teach, it is not enough to have mastered a whole army of languages. To look it at another way, surely there are many unfortunate people who have needed to undergo multiple stomach surgeries. Yet no one would hand a scalpel over to them and ask them to perform the same surgery they received on another person, simply because they themselves had undergone it so often.

If those individuals who conduct surveys and polls had a sense of humor when asking us our occupations, my answer would be "language learner."

Question: Does one need an aptitude to learn so many languages?

Answer: No, it is not necessary. Aside from mastery in the fine arts, success in learning anything is the result of genuine interest and amount of energy dedicated to it. In my own experience learning languages, I have discovered many useful principles. This book outlines them for you.

I wish to acknowledge that my achievement in languages is due to my collaborators over the years, known and unknown. This book is dedicated to them.

—KL, 1970

Foreword to the
Second Edition

≈

THE INTEREST in language learning—not the value of my ideas on the subject—explains why the first edition of this book sold out in a matter of weeks. Once the book was actually read, however, people considered my ideas on language learning to be quite controversial.

In hundreds of letters, newspaper articles, and lectures on college campuses and in language clubs, there have been discussions and arguments regarding the fact that in Hungary we are forced to learn various foreign languages because of our linguistic isolation, and that my book endorses this "forcing." I do not promote the forcing of anything. My view is that knowing languages is part of the process of becoming a cultured person. I am grateful to all those whose remarks and comments have supported my conviction.

Also controversial was my view on the question, "Is there such a thing as an innate ability for learning language(s)?" I don't believe there is. Indeed, one of my goals in writing the book was to remove the mystical fog surrounding the idea of an "innate ability" for language learning. I want to demystify language learning, and to remove the heroic status associated with learning another language.

Apologies to those who have an opposite stance on the subject, for I cannot offer any new argument. I can only reiterate what I stated in the book:

1. Interest driven by motivation, perseverance, and diligence determines one's success in learning a language;

2. An innate ability to learn languages, or rather the qualities that make up this skill, are not possible to find in one person.

Due to lack of time since the publication of the first edition, I can only give thanks to everyone who shared his or her appreciation of my work. My favorite comment may have come from seven-year-old Ildikó, who told me, "When I get to be your age, I will speak many more languages than you—just wait and see!" Another memorable comment came from a Swedish woman, who at over 70 years of age is starting on her eighth language. She invited me to a "translation duel" (terms: who can translate a famous poem most successfully in the least amount of time). Finally, I would like to give thanks to a young writer, Mr. S. Pál, for his view that "The optimism of the writer is the most important point in the book. And we, the readers, from now on will have a more hopeful perspective and are more likely to overcome our original inhibitions and look upon learning a new language as a personal goal of high value, which we can hope to fulfill to the best of our abilities."

"Enthusiasm is contagious," wrote János Selye.

If I have been able to infect only a few people, then I have achieved my purpose with this book.

—KL, 1972

Foreword to the
Fourth Edition

≈

MY BOOK was first published 25 years ago. The quarter century that has passed has been an age of great political and economic fluctuations. Country borders have been born or blurred and complete ethnic groups have set off to find new homelands in new linguistic environments. All this has made it even more important to analyze language-learning methods and to evaluate their efficiency.

My perspective has become broader as well. I have visited new countries and conducted interviews with famous polyglots. I've become acquainted with a branch of a till-now unknown language family. I have looked at the question of whether a language can be easy or difficult, and what the connection is between age and learning ability. This is how the new edition came about: to address some questions not covered in the previous ones.

This new edition has strengthened my conviction that self-assurance, motivation, and a good method play a much more important role in language learning than the vague concept of innate ability, and that dealing with languages is not only an effective and joyful means of developing human relationships, but also of preserving one's mental capacity and spiritual balance.

—*KL, 1995*

Introduction

≈

I MUST have been about four years old when I surprised my family with the declaration that I spoke German.

"How so?" they asked.

"Well, it's like this: if 'lámpa'[5] is *Lampe* and 'tinta'[6] is *Tinte*, then 'szoba'[7] can only be *Sobbe*[8] and 'kályha'[9] must be *Kaiche*.[10]

Had my dear parents been familiar with the jargon of modern linguistics, they would have said: "This poor child has succumbed to the phenomenon of false friends." (This is what we call the type of error committed as a result of mistaken generalizations about another language.) Instead, they grew perplexed and saddened and decided, once and for all, to strike me off the list of those capable of mastering a foreign language.

Initially, life appeared to prove them right. In junior high school, I lagged far behind my classmates who were of German origin or who had had German nannies. Years later, after I got out of high school, I was still regarded, and I regarded myself, as a foreign language flop. So when I applied to college, I set my sights on the natural sciences.

Yet I had already come under the spell of languages. Years before, leafing through my sister's textbooks, I had

---

5. Hungarian: lamp.
6. Hungarian: ink.
7. Hungarian: room.
8. Actually, it is *Zimmer* in German.
9. Hungarian: stove or heater.
10. Actually, it is *Ofen* in German.

come across a page full of Latin proverbs. Though I had not yet studied Latin, I spelled out each beautifully ring-ing sentence and their approximate Hungarian equivalents with great delight: *Juventus ventus...* (Youth is folly...), *Per angusta ad augusta* (All beginnings are difficult). Could it be possible to build with such diamond bricks the thought bridge that spans the space between minds? I fell in love with languages over a few proverbs—folk wisdom crystal-lized into laconic figures of speech.

I insisted that I be enrolled in a French class, taught at the junior high as an extracurricular course. The great advantage of this course was that it was free of charge; its disadvantage was that poor Ms. Budai had been chosen to teach it solely on the basis of her first name: Clarisse. The principal must have thought: "With such a name, the per-son must certainly know French." In any event, both Ms. Budai and I were filled with ambition. I shall never forget that after a month she made me class monitor out of a sense of gratitude. And I, after diligent perusal of the dictionary, inscribed on the blackboard *"La toute classe est bienne..."*[11]

In college, I did poorly in physics and well in chemistry. I was especially fond of organic chemistry. It is my belief to this day that the reason for this was that I had mastered Latin grammar by this time. Knowing how to deduce the entire declension system of nouns and the conjugation of verbs from the simple phrase *agricola arat* (the farmer ploughs) helped me enormously. All I had to do was substitute the hydrogen atoms of the two basic compounds—methane and benzene—with ever-new roots.

Thus, I went to sit for my PhD exam in chemistry with calm assurance, knowing that I would soon have my doc-toral degree in hand. At the same time, I also knew that I would not be able to do much with it; in the early 1930s,

---

11. Incorrect; it is as if one said "*The class whole is well" instead of "The whole class is good" (*Toute la classe est bonne*).

Hungary, like most of the rest of the world, was in a deep economic depression. There we all were, with our spanking new degrees, trying hard to figure out what to do next.

I chose a career for myself quickly: I would make my living teaching languages. The next decision was a bit more difficult: which language would I teach? Latin was not a very sought-after commodity, and there were more French teachers than students in Budapest. English was the only sure and steady breadwinner. But I had to learn it first.

Spurred on by the two incentives of necessity and thirst for knowledge, I worked out a method for language learning that I use to this day. I will devote the forthcoming chapters to it.

Will this method work for others? I shall attempt to answer that question later. At this point, however, I would like to emphasize my conviction that anybody would have reached the same results had they hit their books with the same curiosity and stick-to-it-ness that I did in the spring of 1933, crouched at the end of my living room couch.

I started by intensively studying a novel by Galsworthy. Within a week, I was intuiting the text; after a month, I understood it; and after two months, I was having fun with it.

When I landed my first job teaching English, however, I wanted to teach my students using a more proper, pedagogical approach. Thus I waded through a study course that was popular at the time, called "50 Lessons." I still have no pangs of conscience about having dared to teach a language on the basis of the Latin adage *docendo discimus* (we learn by teaching), treading just one or two lessons ahead of my students. I hope that my energy and enthusiasm made up for what I lacked in linguistic knowledge.

I also tried translating at a pharmaceutical lab where I had managed to get some sort of job.

My translations, however, apparently didn't cut it because the proofreader sent them back with the remark, "Whoever did this must have been one gutsy person!"

I did need real guts for the next step I was about to take, a step that really tied the knot between me and my new profession. In 1941, I decided to learn Russian.

I'd give a lot to be able to write here that it was my political instincts that led me to make this decision, but I can't. All I know is that I took advantage of an incredible opportunity. Browsing in a secondhand bookshop downtown, I came across a two-volume Russian-English dictionary. I made a beeline for the cashier's counter with my treasure. It didn't require much of a sacrifice: I paid pennies for the two musty, ragged volumes that had been published in 1860.

I never put them down after that.

In the early 1940s it was suspicious to study Russian in Hungary, which was becoming more and more fascist. Thus it was downright lucky that I had worked out a method for language learning based on texts. Although there was Russian instruction going on at the university (I believe), for me to get into that program was about as likely as getting a scholarship to study in Russia.

I found a few classic Russian novels in someone's private collection; these I could not tackle. Chance came to my aid once again.

A lot of White Russian émigrés lived in Berlin then. One of these families happened to take a vacation for a few weeks in Balatonszárszó, a small resort on our Lake Balaton. My husband and I happened to take their room at the inn the very day they left, and the maid was just about to dump the stuff they had left behind. In the clutter I discovered, with mounting excitement, a thick book with large Cyrillic lettering: it was a silly, sentimental romance novel from 1910. I set to it without a moment's hesitation. I spent so much time tinkering with it, trying to understand the text, that to this day I still remember certain pages of it word for word.

By the time I was able to move on to more quality reading, it was 1943 and carpet bombings were upon us. As a result of hours spent in the bomb shelter, I was able to progress faster. All I had to do was camouflage my book. I purchased a thick Hungarian encyclopedia and had a book-binder acquaintance sew the pages of Gogol's *Dead Souls* in place of every second sheet. During air raids, I would wade through entire chapters of it. This was the time I worked out my technique of boldly skipping over unfamiliar words, for it would have been dangerous to consult a Russian diction-ary in the bomb shelter.

With the siege raging, I tried to pass the time in the dark cellar by constantly working on the conversation I would have with the first Russian soldier who set foot in it. I decided to embellish each sentence with a few adjecti-val and adverbial participles (my mastery of these was the shakiest). Moreover, I would dazzle him not only with the ease and elegance of my command of his language, but with my literary accomplishments as well: I would draw paral-lels between the poetry of Pushkin and Lermontov; I would sing the praises of Sholokhov's epic style; and so on and so forth.

That was the dream. The reality, in contrast, was that in the sudden quiet of the dawning New Year's Day, I stole up into the bleak and barren garden surrounding the building. Barely had I filled my lungs with a few fresh breaths when a rather young soldier jumped over the fence into the garden. He was clutching a milk jug, making it obvious what he was doing there. But he did utter a few words:

"*Korova est?*" he asked.

I, on the other hand, was so discombobulated with ex-citement that I didn't even recognize the word for "cow." The young man tried to help.

"*Korova! You know? Moo…oo…oo!*"

As I just kept staring at him agape, he shrugged and jumped over the other fence.

The second encounter transpired a few hours later, by which time I had had a chance to get over the first fiasco.

This time a very young man opened the door of the cellar. He asked for salt, then took some bread and bacon out of his rucksack and set to eating comfortably, every once in a while offering us a bite on the point of his jack-knife. When he realized that I spoke Russian, he was greatly moved.

"*Molodets Partisanka!*" (Well done, little guerrilla!) He shook my hand vigorously.

After a while, some Romanian officers entered and I greeted them. (We were liberated at Rákosfalva, where Romanian troops were also stationed.)

"What kind of language are you speaking with those guys?" The Russian soldier said scowling.

"I'm speaking French," I replied.

The little Russ shook his head, then packed up his provisions, stood up, and started out. From the threshold, he hissed back at me: "*Shpionka!*" (Little spy!)

So much for being multilingual!

City Hall was liberated on February 5, 1945. I presented myself that day as a Russian interpreter. They lost no time in hiring me and I received my first assignment right away: I had to call the city commander and tell him who the mayor was. When I asked for the phone number of the commander's headquarters, they just shrugged and told me to pick up the receiver; HQ would be at the other end. There was but one live phone line in Budapest on February 5, 1945.

From that time on, I had no end of opportunities to practice my language skills. The only trouble was that although I was able to gab in Russian fluently (probably with lots of errors), I barely understood anything. My interlocutors attributed this difficulty to a hearing problem. To console me, they sweetly roared into my ear that as soon as my health was restored, my hearing would return as well. At the time, I weighed 44 pounds less than normal for my height.

In January 1946, I was appointed Director of the Metropolitan Office of Tourism. It was a nice title with a good salary; I even had an office of my own in the relatively intact building of the Vigadó.[12] The only fly in the ointment was that no tourist could be found anywhere, high or low, throughout the land. Our roads were all torn up, our bridges sunken into the Danube. Of all our hotels—if I remember correctly—only the one on Margaret Island was open for business. Budapest's need for an Office of Tourism equaled its need for a Colonial Ministry (i.e., there was none).

As we approached spring, my colleagues and I spent our days cutting out pictures from magazines, old and new, and displaying them on the walls of our offices according to this theme: "Past—Present—Future." The past was represented by old street scenes of Pest-Buda before the unification,[13] the future by the plans of reconstruction just being drawn up at the time, and the present by images of shot-up, collapsed buildings.

One day, as I was trying to wend my way through the crowd bustling among the ruined, scaffolded houses along Petőfi Sándor Street,[14] a man made a beeline for me. He asked me, with the French accent of a native speaker, where he could find a post office.

I gave him directions and asked him what had brought him to Budapest. It turned out that curiosity had brought him our way. He was the proverbial first swallow who was meant to bring summer tourists to Hungary.

Without thinking I immediately took him by the arm and dragged him off towards my office.

"I am the manager of a splendid establishment," I said.

---

12. A landmark Budapest exhibition hall and theater, built in the 1860s, comparable to the Met in New York; the name means Merry-making Hall or Entertainment Hall.

13. Budapest was unified and named Budapest in 1873; before then, three "cities" were recognized instead: Pest, on the Eastern bank of the Danube, Buda, on the Western bank, and Óbuda (Old Buda), North of Buda. Together, they were sometimes referred to as Pest-Buda.

14. In the heart of downtown Budapest. This street was named after one of Hungary's greatest 19th-century poets.

"You must pay us a visit at once."

The foreigner attempted to politely extricate himself from my grasp. Embarrassed, he offered the excuse that he was not in the mood and did not have the time besides.

I, however, was not about to be shaken off. "One must make time for such things! I guarantee you will spend a pleasant hour in the company of my colleagues, all ladies who speak French extremely well. Not to mention all the pictures on display that are sure to arouse your interest!"

"But Madame, I am a married man!" That was his last-ditch argument.

I despaired at such obtuseness. "What would become of our profession if we were to limit it to unmarried people?" My companion, however, forcefully pulled himself free of my grasp and disappeared into the crowd.

"And they say that the French are polite!"

I was incensed—until, slowly, I began to see my own stupidity.

When the Allied Commission was set up in Hungary, I was appointed to manage its administrative affairs. One couldn't imagine a more ideal posting for a linguist—and by then, I felt I was one.

I was rapidly alternating between English-, Russian- and French-speaking negotiating partners, switching languages every 10 minutes or so. Not only did my vocabulary receive an immense boost, but I was also able to gain tremendous experience in the skill that is so essential for interpreting: I learned to switch from the linguistic context of one language to another in seconds.

The spirit of linguistic discovery spurred me on and led me next to learn Romanian. To this day, I find Romanian very fetching. It has more of a country flavor than French and is more "manly" than Italian and more interesting than Spanish, due to its Slavic loanwords. This unique blend aroused such enthusiasm in me that I read a Sebastianu novel and László Gáldi's grammar booklets in just weeks. Today I no longer speak Romanian but have plenty of occasions to translate Romanian technical papers into other languages.

My administrative work and my interpreting/translating consumed me fully until 1950. In that year two questions that had been bothering me for a long time became impossible to ignore.

The first was whether the method I had worked out for approaching a foreign language through interesting reading would work for other learners as well. Fortunately, an ideal situation arose to test my theory.

The teaching of Russian in colleges had great momentum in those days, and I was offered a lectureship at the Polytechnic Institute. As the courses were for engineering students, I thought it would be logical to approach the language through their technical expertise and build the edifice of language upon that foundation. The students and I formed a small collaborative group and soon produced two Russian textbooks, emphasizing technical texts. Even with all the errors caused by our inexperience, I am glad to claim this project as my brainchild and I am very glad that the reading of technical texts for language learning has become common practice in all our universities.

The other question that had been nagging at me was what I would do with languages in which I could not rely on analogies with Germanic, Slavic, or Romance languages. Again, a situation arose to address it: that year, at the University's East Asian Institute, a Chinese course was offered for the first time.

I'll give a description of my first encounter with Chinese because I see it as symbolic of my whole relationship to languages—and to learning in general.

It was not easy to get into the course. University students, especially language majors, were given preference, and I was already past the age when people usually embark upon such a major enterprise. And so it happened that I did not receive a reply to my application. Then I found out by chance that the course had already started weeks before.

At around seven o'clock on a fall evening, I found my-self at the university. I groped along its dark corridors, trying to find the lecture hall. I wandered from floor to floor: there was no sign of anyone in the building. I was about to give up and put the whole enterprise on ice when I noticed a thin line of light seeping from under the door of the farthest room at the end of a long, deserted corridor. Although this may sound corny, I believe to this day that it was not the sliver of light shining under the door but the light of my desire for knowledge that overcame the darkness. I entered the hall, introduced myself to the charming lady instructor from Shanghai, and ever since, my life has been lit up by the beauty of Oriental languages.

I spent the next day stooped over the only Chinese-Russian dictionary to be had at any public library, trying to figure out how to transliterate words from Chinese, a language that knows no letters (and hence no alphabet). A few days later, at dawn on a December morning, I set to deci-phering my first Chinese sentence. Well, I worked way into the wee hours of that night until I finally cracked it. The sentence was, "Proletarians of the world, unite!"

In two years I had made such progress in Chinese that I was able to interpret for the Chinese delegations arriv-ing in our country and I was able to translate novels I had grown fond of, one after another. In 1956, I started think-ing about how to make the knowledge I had acquired work for me in another Oriental language. And so I embarked on Japanese—this time, completely alone. The account of my study of that language—a very instructive tale—will be given in detail in another chapter.

Meanwhile, the number of Russian teachers had in-creased to the point where I was able to give up my post to professional educators and start working on another lan-guage, Polish. Classes were announced and students were invited to enroll. When I enrolled, I used a trick that I highly recommend to all my fellow linguaphiles who are serious about learning a language: sign up for a level much higher than what you are entitled to by your actual knowledge. Of the three levels available (beginner's, intermediate, and advanced), I asked to be enrolled at the advanced level.

When the instructor tried to ascertain my level of expertise, I replied, "Don't bother. I don't speak a word of Polish."

"Then why on Earth do you wish to attend an advanced course?" He was astonished.

"Because those who know nothing must advance vigorously."

He got so confused by my tortuous reasoning that he added my name to the class roster without another word.

In 1954 I had the opportunity to travel abroad for the first time. Although I have traipsed across just about the whole globe since then, I have never been as excited as the day I found out that I would be able to go on a package tour to Czechoslovakia with the Hungarian Travel Agency (IBUSZ). As an act of gratitude, I immediately bought Ivan Olbracht's novel *Anna the Proletarian*. By perusing it with my by-then customary method, I unlocked the secrets of Czech declensions and conjugations. I made notes of the rules I gleaned in the book's margins. The poor book deteriorated to such a degree as a result of this heartless treatment that it fell apart the minute I got home.

My knowledge of Italian has less lofty origins. In the early 1940s, a brave craftsman tried to sell some Italians the patent rights to a machine that manufactured shoe uppers. Even after diligent perusal of the dictionary, my translation must have been more persuasive than objective, for the Italians bought the patent rights without further inquiry.

My relationship with Spanish is of more recent origin. I blush to acknowledge that I embarked on it by reading the Spanish translation of a silly American bestseller, *Gentlemen Prefer Blondes*. By the time I was finished with it, all I needed to do was verify the rules of accidence and syntax I had gleaned. Rudolf Király's grammar reference served this purpose well.

By the late 1960s, Budapest had developed into a city of conferences, and I became more and more interested in interpreting. In the coming chapters, there will be more on the subject of interpreting, which in my opinion is the most interesting of all intellectual professions. What still belongs here in the Introduction is mention of the fact that my very first "live performance" brought success: one of the delegates at my first conference in Budapest asked me whether I would be amenable to interpreting at a West German conference. I happily accepted. And when I received the written invitation, I thought it would be good manners to learn the language of my hosts.

And so it was that my language-learning career came full circle back to German, its less than glamorous starting point.

1

What Is Language?

≈

THERE MAY be no other word that has as many con-
notations as this noun does with its few letters.

Because the word for "language" in Hungarian is the
same as the word for "tongue," the Hungarian anatomist,
upon hearing it, will think not of human communication
but of the set of muscle fibers divided into root, body, blade,
and tip. The Hungarian gourmet will think of tasty morsels
in stewed, pickled, and smoked forms on the menu, and
the theologian will be reminded of the day of red Pentecost.
The Hungarian writer will think of a tool that dare not rival
Nature,[15] and the poet will imagine a musical instrument.

Those dealing with language for a living are usually
called linguists or philologists. They come up with theories
of language and study the connections between language
and culture.

Those dealing with languages as a vocation or hobby
have no name in Hungarian. It is a bit ironic because these
people love languages, learn them easily, and speak them
well. The English language has a word for such people: linguaphiles. I feel that a philologist or linguist is to a lingua-

---

15. Reference to a poem by Sándor Petőfi: "Oh Nature, glorious Nature,
who would dare / with reckless tongue to match your wondrous fare?"
("The Tisza," translated by Watson Kirkconnell.)

phile what a choreographer is to a ballerina.

So our subject is the linguaphile, the person who wishes to acquire a language with the goal of actually using it. If we should still wander to the field of theory, it may be because a linguaphile is an open-eyed, educated person who is usually interested in the broader background of his or her studies. Also, I believe that the right choice of the language to be learned and its effective acquisition is made easier by an overall view. Of course, I realize that linguists and philologists may find my perspective too simplified, and linguaphiles may find it too theoretical.

2

Why Do We and Why Should We Study Languages?

≈

LET'S START with these two basic questions.

I'll begin with the second because it's easier to answer.

We should learn languages because language is the only thing worth knowing even poorly.

If someone knows how to play the violin only a little, he will find that the painful minutes he causes are not in proportion to the possible joy he gains from his playing. The amateur chemist spares himself ridicule only as long as he doesn't aspire for professional laurels. The man somewhat skilled in medicine will not go far, and if he tries to trade on his knowledge without certification, he will be locked up as a quack doctor.

Solely in the world of languages is the amateur of value. Well-intentioned sentences full of mistakes can still build bridges between people. Asking in broken Italian which train we are supposed to board at the Venice railway station is far from useless. Indeed, it is better to do so than to remain uncertain and silent and end up back in Budapest rather than in Milan.

Linguists have written a lot on the first question: why we learn languages. The chief focus, motivation, is such a central problem that a six-day conference was devoted to it in Germany a couple of years ago. Simply, we are motivated to do something when we accept what is necessary to achieve it. To use a metaphor, the Russian language is a complicated, massive cathedral harmoniously fashioned in every arch and corner. The learner must accept this in order to have sufficient motivation to build it. In contrast, the Italian language, praised as easy to learn, has a simpler structure and a more lucid floorplan; but, if any detail is skimped in its construction, it will collapse. We must accept this in order to be motivated to learn the language.

Not long ago, I heard the following story from the mother of a small child. Pete received a whistle, a drum, and a trumpet for his birthday. Pete asked if he could hang each of his toys one by one on the wall of his room.

"We can't," his mom said. "The local government will punish us if we drive so many nails into the wall."

"Why drive them?" the child said. "I don't need the inside part of the nails. I only need the part that juts out!"

I am always reminded of little Pete whenever I hear of someone who is "learning" a language passively. Knowledge—like a nail—is made load-bearing by being driven in. If it is not driven deep enough, it will break when any weight is put upon it.

The building of language has four large halls. Only those who have acquired listening, speaking, reading, and writing can declare themselves to be its dwellers. Those wanting to inhabit these halls will have to overcome obstacles just as the mythological heroes did. Like Odysseus, they will have to defeat the Cyclops of "I can't remember it again" and resist the Siren's song of "there is a good program on TV." The comparison is, however, not precise. The cunning Greek was able to defeat every challenge through his desire for home— his motivation. For us, the passage through the building of language alone will bring its own joy and motivation, if we tackle the task in a sensible and prudent way.

3

The Type of Language
to Study

≈

THE CHOICE is very wide. According to the Bible, foreign languages were born when God destroyed the Tower of Babel. When it collapsed, 72 languages appeared: this many because Noah's three sons had 72 descendants. Shem had 26, Ham had 32, and Japheth had 14.

The number of descendants and languages alike has considerably increased. As far as the latter is concerned, the German weekly *Der Spiegel* provides rough data (vol. 46, 1994): the inhabitants of our globe communicate with each other in 6000 languages. Where the number of languages has decreased, the explanation is interesting:

> "With the rise of Western culture on a given continent, the number of languages used by the inhabitants decreases proportionately. 4900 of our 6000 languages are in Africa and Asia. The population of New Guinea communicate with each other in 800 different languages; those living in Europe and the Middle East only in 275."

According to the article, English is the most widespread language. However, the authors don't put it down to linguistic imperialism but to the development of history and the fact that English is relatively easy to acquire.

The exact number of spoken languages can't be known. In the spectrum of languages, we can only symbolically differentiate between seven main colors; in practice, the individual colors fade into each other through a number of hues. The way from Italian towards French leads through Ligurian and Provençal; if I like, I can consider them as four distinct languages; if I like, I can consider one a dialect of Italian and the other a dialect of French.

In the spectrum of languages, there have always been those glittering with a more blinding light: the so-called world languages. These are the ones with a larger "radius of action"; these are the ones that tried to attract the humbler ones into their magic circle. They never completely succeeded, not even Latin, which in the Roman Empire stretched from Dacia through Iberia. My witness is Ovid.

The pampered duke of poets fell out of favor with his majestic patron, Emperor Augustus, and was banned from Rome for some court gossip. The poet had to leave the metropolis, glittering with light, for Tomis, inhabited by the dregs of the Empire. Yet Ovid, the uncrowned king of Latin, didn't suffer most for the shame of exile but for not knowing the vernacular of the local population.

Barbarus hic ego sum, quia non intellegor ulli. (Here *I'm* the barbarian no one comprehends.)

His sigh may well be translated but hardly understood. Today, when a considerable part of most countries' Gross National Product is provided by tourism, the Western visitor is surrounded by locals trying to offer him accommodation not in their language but in his.

4

"Easy" and "Difficult" Languages

≈

I PUT the adjectives above in quotes not because I question the idea that languages are different in their learnability. Instead, I've done it to suggest that the question we should be asking is: "For whom is a language easy and for whom is it difficult?"

Everyone acquires their mother tongue commensurate to their own level of verbal intelligence. However, as far as foreign languages are concerned, Herre Borquist from Stockholm will learn within days how to make himself understood in Norwegian, Signore Pirrone will fare easily in Spanish, and Pyotr Petrovich will get by in Ukrainian. Considering the whole issue, there are general criteria on how easily languages can be learned which I'd like to comment on from the perspective of a polyglot…

Every language is a code system. It is not like the one used in diplomacy, which often changes according to the situation. Instead, a language resembles the traffic code, which is permanent and easy to understand. Red commands us to stop in all regions of the world. Green tells us to proceed. Arrows show the direction of traffic.

Languages, too, have their international codes: punctuation marks. The period denotes the end of a sentence, the comma its continuation. The question and exclamation mark are obvious.

However, the universality of the code ceases at this point. One has to acquire the phonetics, vocabulary, and grammar for each and every language separately. We can say *rule, pattern, paradigm,* or even *subroutine* or *program*. I prefer the term *shoemaker's last*—so I will stick to my last.

A language is more difficult the more lasts we need within it to form (1) meaningful words from sounds/letters; and (2) sentences from words.

The trouble of grammatical manipulation of words doesn't really exist in Chinese. When I was in China several decades ago, the slogan "Books to the People" was in fashion. It was visible on the walls of every house in the form of four decorative hieroglyphs. The exact translation is "Take book give people." The Chinese seemed to understand it: I'd never seen so many men absorbed in newspapers and so many children crouching over their books as in Mao's country.

The study of Chinese and Japanese is, in theory, made easier by the fact that some of the characters are ideograms (i.e., the character's form reveals its meaning). In alphabetic languages, it only applies to a couple of onomatopoetic words (clap, splash, knock[16]) and some verbs imitating animal sounds (roar, croak, bleat[17]). It is interesting that reduplicated forms, which are common in Hungarian (*csip-csup,*[18] *kip-kop,*[19] *tik-tak*[20]), occur less frequently in other languages and are mostly of a belittling or mocking nature, like *riff-raff* (lower-class); *tittle-tattle* (idle gossip); the German *Mischmasch* (hodgepodge); the French *charivari* (hullaba-

---

16. The Hungarian equivalents are *csattan, csobban,* and *koppan.*
17. The Hungarian equivalents are *béget* (for sheep), *brekeg* (for frogs), and *mekeg* (for goats).
18. Hungarian: petty, measly, trifling.
19. Hungarian: knock-knock, pit-a-pat, rat-a-tat.
20. Hungarian: tick-tack (a ticking or tapping beat like that of a clock).

loo); and the Hebrew *lichluch* (dirt), *bilbel* (confusion), and *kishkush* (scrawl).

Apart from these playful forms, one has to learn not only the connection between sound and meaning but also the link between sound and writing. Good dictionaries provide information on both.

If few lasts are necessary to determine the connection between sounds and letters, we call the language phonetic. We Hungarians feel our mother tongue is like that. The spelling that we acquired in elementary school is so much fixed in us that we don't even notice we pronounce *tudja*[21] "tuggya" and *tartsd*[22] "tardzsd." I only became aware of the diversity of our sounds when I heard a German student of Hungarian wailing about how difficult it was for him to distinguish between *pártalan, páratlan, parttalan, pártatlan, párttalan.*[23] It's also easy to get confused among the words *megörült, megőrült, megürült, megőrölt...*[24]

And all these are within one language! But if we learn foreign languages, we have to familiarize ourselves with the fact that although the word "vice" means the same in many other languages as in Hungarian,[25] it is pronounced in French as "vees," in English as "vis," in Italian as "vee-chay," and is written in German as "Vize."

---

21. Hungarian: he/she knows it (indicative) or he/she should know it (subjunctive); d + j are pronounced as one long sound, the one normally written as *ggy*.

22. Hungarian: you should hold it (subjunctive); t + s are pronounced as one sound, the one normally written as *dzs*, as a result of voicing before the last letter d.

23. *Pár*: pair, couple; *párt*: (political) party; *part*: shore, coast, bank; *-talan* and *-atlan*: privative suffixes. Hence: *pártalan*: uncoupled (uncommon); *páratlan*: odd (number), unparalleled; *parttalan*: boundless, shoreless; *pártatlan*: impartial; *párttalan*: non-partisan.

24. *Megörült*: he/she became happy; *megőrült*: he/she went crazy; *megürült*: it became vacant; *megőrölt*: he/she ground sth.

25. The meaning "substitute" is meant here. The Hungarian word is pronounced "vee-tse" and today is obsolete.

As far as being phonetic is concerned, English gets the worst grade. We get used to the fact that in Hamlet's famous utterance "To be or not to be," the long /i/ sound is written "e." But it is written "ee" in the word "bee," "ea" in the word "leaf," "ie" in the word "siege," and "ey" in the word "key."

I envy musicians! A sequence of sounds—like *Für Elise*—is played the same way today by, say, a skilled Albanian pianist as it was by a skilled English pianist in the 19th century. The connection between a piece of sheet music and a tune is eternal and international, but the relationship between writing and sound varies by language. It is determined, among other things, by the alphabets of languages.

This variability can be deceptive. Once I was in a restaurant in Berlin. The menu offered an attractive-sounding dish: *Schtschie*. I wasn't able to resist, so I ordered it. Only when it was served did I realize that the food that I assumed to be an exotic sort of fish was nothing but the national dish of Russia, щи (*shchi*) (cabbage soup).

Therefore, when studying a language, we have to get acquainted with the lasts so we can encode sounds into letters or produce sounds from letters. Parallel with this, we launch two other processes: the building of sounds/letters into words and the building of words into sentences.

I like the metaphor of construction because we must know how to choose the appropriate words and put them together, i.e. make sentences. There are three major types of "joining operations," based on whether the language is isolating, agglutinative, or inflecting.[26]

In theory, isolating languages appear to be the simplest of the three: words can be placed next to each other in their dictionary forms. Agglutinative languages, on the other hand, require that we "glue" a suffix to the dictionary form of a word when making sentences. (The term comes from

---

26. Isolating languages are also known as analytic languages and inflecting languages as fusional languages.

the Latin word *gluten* [glue].) With inflecting languages, we must inflect (or "bend") the dictionary form of the word depending on its placement in a sentence.

According to historical linguists, articulated speech was born 100,000 years ago. The number of its users has multiplied to several billions since. It would be a miracle if the above three language types were still sharply distinct. English was once an agglutinative language but now is closer to the typically isolating Chinese than the Indo-European languages with which it is classified. Frederick Bodmer, the great philologist, has noted that the English of Alfred the Great (871–901) was a typically inflecting language, and that Anglo-American is predominantly isolating.

I don't know how a foreign student of Hungarian relates to this question but the word *átengedhetnélek* is certainly easier for us than its (longer) equivalent in other languages (e.g., "I could let you go through" [English], *ich könnte dich durchgehen lassen* [German], or я мог бы пропустить тебя [*ya mog by propustit' tebya*] [Russian]).

An advantage of Finno-Ugric (or rather, Uralic) languages is that they don't have the concept of grammatical gender. This is in marked contrast to Semitic languages, which show different forms depending on the genus even when using numbers. In Hebrew, if you are compelled to use the form "not knowing sth" (alas, how often it happens!), in the case of the classic negative particle, *en*, you have to choose the right form out of 10 (!) options, depending on gender and number. The healthy linguistic instinct has even changed it for the gentler negative particle *lo* in everyday speech.

Fewer lasts are necessary in some languages. In English, one can form the plural of nouns by adding a single -*s* (apart from a minimal number of exceptions). Conjugations use this -*s* as well, in the third person singular in the present tense. However, the lack of suffixes makes the word order stricter. If we were to translate *Túrót eszik a cigány*[27] into English, the result could easily be "The cheese is eating the gypsy."

German grammar is difficult. As opposed to the single declension last in English, Előd Halász's dictionary has no choice but to list 49 (!) different forms. German verbs have numerous prefixes, just as Hungarian verbs do. However, both languages are a bit fraudulent, so to speak. For example, although the prefix *ver-* seems to be as innocent as the Hungarian *el-* or *meg-*,[28] it is not: *meiden* and *vermeiden* both mean "to avoid,"[29] yet *kaufen* and *verkaufen* mean "to buy" and "to sell"; *lernen* and *verlernen* mean "to study" and "to forget"; and *sagen* and *versagen* mean "to say" and "to fail." And let's be careful with *sprechen*, too, so that it doesn't become a *Versprecher* (a slip of the tongue)!

It's no use learning dialects. Nor is it useful to learn idiomatic phrases, because they are the spoiled children of language and they change as rapidly as teenagers' slang. However, we must know *sociolects!*[30] They play an important role in Hungarian. We address our older or socially higher-ranking partners in the third person, as if they weren't present: *Professzor úr tart ma előadást?*[31]

---

27. Hungarian: "The gypsy is eating (cottage) cheese," the beginning line of a folk song, usually translated into English as "See the Gypsy Eat Cheese." In this Hungarian sentence, the object comes first (indicated by the *-t*), then the verb, and then finally the subject.

28. Hungarian: *el-* means "away" and *meg-* is a perfective suffix (cf. "eat" and "eat up").

29. Their Hungarian equivalents similarly differ only in a prefix: *kerülni* vs. *elkerülni*.

30. A variety of a language used by a particular social group.

31. Hungarian: "Will you be holding a lecture today?" (to a professor), lit., "Will the professor be holding a lecture today?" Using "professor" instead of "you" is preferred because out of the two formal options for "you," *ön* can sound too distancing or official and *maga* too personal or intimate. The use of third person forms is possible because the formal second-person conjugation is the same as the one in the third person.

The study of sociolects is often not about grammar but word choice. There was a case where a high-ranking diplomat from an exotic country married a Hungarian woman. They had a child, and the woman sometimes talked with their child in Hungarian. This is the only way I can explain the fact that when a member of our government visited him in his office, the diplomat offered a seat to him thusly: *"Csüccs!"*[32]

In Japan, the predominant sociolect requires a level of politeness and deference that can seem excessive when compared to other languages. For example, a waiter is required to talk to a customer like this: *"O-mizu-o omochi itashimasho-ka?"* (Sir, may I please serve you some water?). The standard answer to the question "How are you?" is *"O-kage sama de genki des."* (Because of you, I am fine.)

---

32. Hungarian: "sit down" in child language. The proper expression is *"Foglaljon helyet!"*

5

How to Study Languages

≈

"HOW CAN I learn English, Russian, French, German, Spanish (delete as appropriate)?" I often hear this question.

The most secure and painless way to the perfect mastery of, let's say, German is being born a German.

Well, it's a bit late for that. Some missed it by 10 years, some by 20 or 30, but all of us missed this opportunity of a lifetime.

Another solution is that one can live in a German-speaking region, possibly in one's youth and for an extended period of time.

This is a somewhat more feasible way but not easily viable, either.

A third solution is that we take two or more classes a week regularly and industriously, and after four or five years, we reach the level of knowledge that satisfies our own high standards.

The goal of this book is not to substitute but to complement this most common way of language learning, considered classic. I would not say my book offers "suggestions" or "recipes" for all the money in the world. I would simply like to tell how I, over 25 years, got to the point of being able to speak 10 languages, translate technical documents and enjoy fiction in six more, and read journalism in 11 more or so.

To reach true fluency in 10 languages, I would have needed at least 60 years using classic methods, since among the languages I learned are such "difficult" languages as Chinese and Japanese. (The quotation marks are not around the adjective to suggest that these two languages aren't difficult but because there is no "easy" language. At most, some languages may be easier to learn poorly.)

I have not found the magic password that springs open the lock on the gate of knowledge. One of the reasons is that there is no such password. If I still wish to relate my experience, I only do so because during this half-century, study has never been a burden for me but always an inexhaustible source of joy.

I wouldn't have written this book if I felt that my relationship with language learning was an individual peculiarity. It is because I believe that my way is viable for all those thirsty for knowledge and ready for intellectual adventures that I transmit the conclusions I have drawn.

There are language learners whose lack of motivation or pressing schedule restricts their progress. My book is not for them. I have no doubt that they will be educated by our professional—and competent—teachers. By transmitting my humble experience, I would like to increase the joy of learning and reduce its difficulties for those who are not satisfied by the pace of teachers.

6

Who This Book Is
and Isn't For

≈

MY BOOK was written for the kind of person who doesn't really exist. the Average Language Learner.

Being "average" is the most abstract and rare thing in the world. Whenever I read statistical reports, I try to imagine my unfortunate contemporary, the Average Person, who, according to these reports, has 0.66 children, 0.032 cars, and 0.046 TVs.

Yet, it was the Average Language Learner I had in mind when I was conceiving my book. Hence, it is indispensable to delineate him or her more closely.

His or her age is between 16 and 96. His or her profession can be whatever: a university student, a gardener, a dentist, a seamstress, or a retired chief accountant. There are two disqualifying criteria: too much and too little free time.

I will insert two questions here that arise almost every time I give a talk: what is the best age to begin learning a foreign language, and what is the oldest age when one can still do so?

The first question concerns mainly parents and the second one pensioners looking for a useful pastime.

Let's start with the first question.

I will cite an experiment that involved swimming lessons for babies. The conductors of the experiment observed that babies two weeks old would frolic uninhibited in basins suited to their size. It was theorized that the babies still had in their neurons the memory of the months spent in the amniotic fluid. But at six months, the babies would not submerge themselves uninhibited in the water; they had grown used to the phenomenon of air.

This is more or less the case with language as well. The mother tongue is inhibition and prejudice. I have seen four- or five-year-old children stamping their feet in anger and even threatening with their fists the person who speaks like a human but is incomprehensible.

The usual argument against the playful method of foreign language instruction that is started before prejudices can set in is "the child won't learn either language very well." To be frank, I have never seen an example of that in my life. If that were the case, the bilingual children raised at the borders and those raised by nannies would all be idiots.

My objection to early foreign language instruction, especially by relatives, is that it's rarely effective. As far as a child is concerned, a mother, father, or grandparent is already inseparable from his or her mother tongue. Yet if one parent is a native speaker of a language foreign to the environment, let him or her make use of the opportunity to teach a still pliable mind. The result may come out only years later, when the child begins learning the foreign language consciously and with motivation, but it is still something.

I emphasize the native foreign language of the instructing parent because youth is the age of the unconscious development of skills; in language learning, it is the period of mechanical imitation of foreign sounds. Beyond a certain age (usually 12 to 14 years), one generally cannot acquire native-like pronunciation.

I don't recommend my method to those who have too much or too little free time.

If one can devote an unlimited number of hours to language learning, a concentrated program can be followed; such programs are outside the scope of this book. If, on the other hand, one can't devote even 60–90 minutes a day to language learning, this book is not suitable either. My book is for the average language learner.

Also, a certain interest is required beyond the practical problems of language learning, as well as a bit of healthy impatience with the pace of learning dictated by the old, decent, and regular methods. This is because the age in which we live demands some acceleration of learning as well.

Any method of language instruction is a construction. It is characteristic of the age in which it was born.

The aim of my book doesn't require—and its length doesn't permit—complicated elaborations on the social sciences. Let me then just rephrase the previous paragraph into the language of pedagogy: historically, the language-learning methods that come to the fore in every age suit the social demands of the period.

How do these demands change over time?

In this short review of the history of language learning, I will start with the Romans, because language learning begins with them. This is where the biggest, eternal glory of our trade lies.

It was just a language—the Greek language with its higher culture—that caused the Romans, intoxicated by their military conquests, to first lay down their arms.

> *Graecia capta ferum victorem cepit et artes*
> *intulit agresti Latio*

> (Captive Greece took captive her fierce conqueror, and introduced her arts into rude Latium.)

> Horace: Epistles, II, 1
> (Translated by C. Smart)

Victorious Rome pounced on the established culture of Greece with the greed of the nouveau riche. To appropriate it, she chose a way suited to the age. She put the captured Greeks into war chariots rolling towards Latium—or made them trudge behind in chains. And so it came to be that Roman youths were taught Greek by Greek prisoners of war.

The fate of our first fellow language teachers was not enviable. They were only allowed to communicate with their Roman masters as long as their students produced something. When the *adolescens Romanus,* the Roman youth with black locks and aquiline nose, grew bored of his lessons, his teacher suffered the same limitation of speech as his fellow slaves.

Over time, the Romans enriched the world with no less magnificent works of art than the Greeks had. The knowledge of Latin became a symbol in the feudal world—a symbol of belonging to the privileged class. (In today's American language, one would call it a status symbol.) This means of social division was used—as always—to suppress all underprivileged classes. Women were rarely allowed to study Latin or Greek. (Nobles' wives sulk in Mikszáth's[33] short stories that their men speak Latin, excluding them from the conversation.)

It is understandable, therefore, that at the birth of capitalism, the rising middle class adopted language learning as a social springboard. By learning the two classical languages, the middle class hoped to elevate themselves socially as well as dissociate themselves from the other classes not speaking them. This was when the gymnasium[34] was born. Its curriculum was designed completely around the instruction of these two languages.

One of the purposes of teaching Latin and Greek was

---

33. Kálmán Mikszáth, Hungarian writer of the 19th century.
34. A type of secondary school that prepares pupils for university.

for discipline. This mentality, based on having pupils cram grammar, suited very well the barracks' atmosphere of German boarding schools and the system of English public schools that often led to sadism. Is it by chance that the word "discipline" has a double meaning: "a field of study" and "orderly conduct"?

The fact that the first really large-scale, language-learning operations involved two dead languages determined the method of instruction for a long time. This was unfortunate because it was out of the question for the pupil to feel the linguistic elements as handy tools or building blocks to be used for communication at his or her discretion (which is emphasized so much today). It took a century for schools to become liberated from this burden.

Because the voices of our ancestors who lived before Christ were not recorded by any electronic device, it is understandable that pronunciation problems have never been systematically addressed in pedagogy. To my knowledge, the debate over pronunciation hasn't been decided even today. In England, the names of Caesar and Cicero are taught as /kaisar/ and /kikero/, which we Hungarians are used to hearing as /tsaysar/ and /tsitsero/. By the way, it was England that insisted on the instruction of classical languages the longest and the most stubbornly. It was in the parliamentary minutes that when a lord got stuck in the middle of a Latin quotation, all the upper house rose as one person and continued the quotation.

The fact that Britain reveres tradition is not the only reason why Latin and Greek have been in the curricula of English schools for so long. English orthography (spelling), having little connection with pronunciation, can be learned more easily by pupils if they have some idea of classical languages. "Ocean," which sounds like /oh-shn/, and "theatre," perceived as /thietuh/, are easier to write down if one has the words *oceanus/okeanos* and *theatrum/theatron* behind him.

Until around the mid-19th century, due to aristocrats' marriages spreading over borders and the ensuing settlements and blending, urban citizenry spoke "foreign" languages. The turn towards broader language instruction took place at the end of the century when the interest in living languages became greater than what could be satisfied by geographical or family circumstances. Wanderers who set off down the highway with a bundle on their backs and a tool in their pockets were guided not only by the spirit of adventure and the hope for a bigger piece of bread, but also by the desire for learning languages. The system of "exchange children," too, was born to satisfy this need.

The mail coach was replaced by the train, and the sailing ship by the steamship. Countries got closer to each other and interest in peoples beyond the borders became keener. The developing trade relations involved a new motivation as well, and this new motivation called for a new form of knowledge—that of living, spoken, and everyday languages. The age was ripe for the birth of a more modern language-learning method. Soon Mr. Berlitz appeared on the scene and then his many followers.

The essence of Berlitz's method is making a connection between an object (concept) and its foreign-language name without the mother tongue mediating, e.g., "This is a book, that is a pencil."

When the shipwrecked protagonist in Karinthy's *Capillaria*[35] got before the queen of the depths of the seas, this was the method he used when trying to attract her attention: "By the method of the excellent Mr. Berlitz, I pointed at myself and I said: 'human.'"

This method, the direct method, dethroned translation among private language teachers. In schools, however, translation continued as the basis for language teaching in vari-

---

35. A fantasy novel written by Frigyes Karinthy, a Hungarian writer of the early 20th century, first published in English in 1965.

ous, gradually modernizing forms.

By this time in Europe (late 19th century), boys and girls at the age of 10 were starting to learn foreign languages in school. By the time they reached secondary school, they had some knowledge of one or even two foreign languages. But being drilled with grammar and forced to memorize exceptions that occur once in a leap-year… no wonder that children left secondary schools with almost no practical language knowledge after studying German for six or eight years. It was only the children of the well-off citizenry who obtained a usable command of a language, as a result of the parents' financial generosity (nannies, tutors) and the children's investment of time.

The nanny system—which is actually rather efficient from the point of view of language learning—is not dissimilar in concept from how the Romans used their Greek captives as teachers. The task of nannies—those exploited domestic maids-of-all-work—was not only language instruction, but also the teaching of manners. I am biased towards these pioneer practitioners of our trade because they were the champions of women's emancipation, fighting amidst much hardship, and because they were the ones who carried and passed on the baton of a higher culture in their philistine environment.

In the mid-20th century, a new generation grew up which related differently to foreign languages than those who were young between the two world wars. The objective and the motivation had changed once again.

Up to this time, the knowledge of a language was part of general knowledge and the ambition to acquire it usually stopped when the student became a worker.

The language-learning needs of the post-Cold War generation, however, do not end with the years in school, and the new generation's objectives do not allow for long-term, leisurely study. The world has shrunk further. Contacts with foreigners are no longer the privilege of professional diplomats, merchants seeking new markets, or boredom-banishing globetrotters. During your everyday work and everyday leisure, you meet speakers of other languages plenty of times: self-interest, curiosity, and expressions of friendship demand that you should learn as quickly as possible how to have a word with them. But it is also the development of technology that has radically changed people's relationship with learning.

We who fly from Budapest to Vienna in one hour instead of riding overland by wagon (three days), and who get light by flipping a switch instead of priming a gas-lamp, will need such immediate methods in language learning as well.

And we have grown comfortable. We expect technology to relieve our physical and spiritual discomforts. In regards to language learning, the audiovisual method tries to reduce the burden arising from the memorization indispensable to any language learning by an increased involvement of the eyes and the ears.

Yet in fairness some new methods help us to acquire an extremely important aspect of communication: good pronunciation.

Even the brave linguaphiles who employed the direct method found it more important to faultlessly gabble the conjugation of *concevoir* and other hardly-ever used verbs in hardly-ever used tenses than to pronounce the language as it is spoken. This is where the audiovisual method, based on image and sound impressions, was expected to do wonders and it did lead to very good results.

The great advantage of the method is the opportunity to repeat the material frequently. And I must stress that repetition is as an essential element of language learning as a knife is to a lathe or fuel is to an internal combustion engine. This primitive truth was, by the way, invented earlier than the gasoline engine: *Repetitio est mater studiorum*—"repetition is the mother of studies"—as our ancestors said.

It is much to the liking of the complacent child that

our schools' educational methods appeal to as many senses as possible. Indeed, it relieves the child's mind of conscious concentration. In the schools of the 19th century, learning grammar was an end to itself. Now, however, we are starting to claim that it is not even precious, not even interesting, to consciously know the regularities of language. It is not worth the trouble to mobilize the mind to learn them. This is the principle the immersion method is based on. It is not by chance that it was born in America, which is so fond of comfort. Oftentimes, the foreign language patterns are taught by excessive repetition, namely multi-hour drills every day, *without revealing any theoretical connections.* Thinking is a sin that only hinders success, promoters believe. Course developers can't comprehend students who, instead of mechanically absorbing the material, show an intellectual resistance.

Yet a grammar rule, like the agreement of adjectives with nouns in French, can be learned by making your mind aware: in the feminine, usually an *-e* is added to the masculine adjective. But it is conceivable—and it takes much less brainwork—that when you hear so many times *"le parc, le champ, le jardin est **grand**"* (the park, the field, the garden is large) and *"la maison, la salle, la chambre est **grande**"* (the house, the hall, the room is large) that in the end, as a result of continuous drill, the correct way of agreement automatically develops in you. Yet you are not aware of it, and therefore cannot build on your knowledge in any intellectual way.

A complacent brain shows smaller resistance to repetition that drizzles like lukewarm rain than to the requirement of conscious concentration. I suspect that this is what sticks the young in front of our TV screens today.

No one disputes the education-spreading effect of this great technological achievement. It is not a mission of this book to speak about what TV programs mean for villagers and shut-ins. It cannot be denied, however, that TV doesn't only draw young people away from reading in terms of time. Images are easier to follow than letters; the lazy imagination reacts more quickly to moving pictures than still ones; and moving pictures with sound require the least investment of intellectual energy. We obtain experiences at the cost of minimal physical—and even less intellectual—effort. Our youth, with a few honorable exceptions, don't read enough.

Even if we, the generation raised on books, view the effects of cinema, radio, and TV with anxiety in this respect, we must admit that these technological achievements are of enormous help in spreading culture, which can promote language learning. <u>It cannot be emphasized too strongly that the main purpose of language learning is to enable communication between speakers of different vernaculars, and technology can facilitate this</u>. For example, to understand your partner's speech and to express your own thoughts correctly, the radio and tape recorder can be of great help. These of course are the inventions employed by the audiovisual method.

We cannot have any objection to their use; at most, we can have some misgivings. We may feel that the problem of language learning is not entirely solved by these means. "There is no royal way to wisdom," as they say.

> Let's stop for a minute and examine a frequently heard delusion. As they say, adults should learn foreign languages the same way they acquired their mother tongue.

I cannot accept this assertion. There is as little likelihood of squeezing an adult into the intellectual framework of their childhood as there is into their first pair of pajamas.

One of the characteristics of children is that they haven't yet learned how to speak. Even the word *infant* (baby) comes from the compound *in-fant* (not speaking).

When babies do start speaking, they grow acquainted with the objects around them and their names at the same time. The outside world unfolds before them slowly and gradually. They learn how to speak because they are compelled to do so by their vital needs (the most powerful motivation!). They must make themselves understood so they can have their needs satisfied.

Adult language learners, however, have a rich intellectual and emotional world to convey. In addition, Pavlov's second signal system—the linguistic form—has already developed in them. To transform this whole, ready signal system into a foreign language can be daunting.

To wit: my teacher friend escaped the Arrow Cross terror, hiding with a pupil of hers; they experienced the liberation together.[36] In mere weeks the little 10-year-old girl was chattering happily with the Soviet officers who lived in the same courtyard, while my friend had great difficulties in conversation. "It's easy for little Eve," she consoled herself, "she only has to translate the knowledge of four grades of elementary school, but I have to translate secondary school and even university in myself first."

Children's and adults' abilities differ from each other. A child is automatic; an adult is logical. I saw an illustrative example of this trivial truth not long ago at an examination of first-graders. The seven-year-old ladies and gentlemen recited various poetic and prosaic texts from memory for 15 minutes, which was a piece of cake for their young minds. These same children's lips, however, became completely mute when the teacher asked them a question in connection with a poem: "Why do you say that the cow is a domestic animal?" In the end a girl with a blonde braid saved the prestige of the class: "Because it is not wild," she replied.

It is a bitter lesson but it has to be expressed once: the time spent on language learning is lost unless it reaches a

---

36. The Arrow Cross Party was a fascist organization that was in power in 1944–1945 in Hungary; it executed many thousands of Jews. The Soviet "liberation" (and occupation) was completed by April 1945.

certain—daily and weekly—concentration.

Serious people tend to avoid generalizations, but one claim seems appropriate here: the average language learner needs to study a minimum of 10–12 hours a week. If one cannot or doesn't want to invest this much time, he or she should think twice about the enterprise.

(An interesting question is if someone who invests, say, four times as much on learning will be able to acquire lasting knowledge in a fourth of the time.)

The 10–12 hours a week is, of course, an average. Still, let's start from this average when we look at the language-learning method of a working adult.

According to the old, classic division of a day, one devotes eight hours to working, eight to resting or recreation, and eight to sleeping.

Hypnotists tried to use the eight hours for sleep for language learning. The attempt was unsuccessful and was discontinued.

I cannot comment on the psychological basis of the relaxation method, which has a growing popularity, due to my lack of technical knowledge. I find its material, which is recorded on tape with enviable, beautiful pronunciation, well structured. I only miss two things about it—my two fixed ideas.

One is being *interesting*. We know that its meaning is "being inside, being within" *(inter esse)*. This is the secret of radio and TV quiz shows. The viewers/listeners spontaneously become involved in the game: they compete together with the participants and they test their own knowledge. Persistent attention—one of the preconditions of all successful learning—is assured.

The language-learning tape one listens to tells one, "This is how you should say it." In the adult mind, however, a question inevitably arises: "*Why* should I say it like that?" And if one can find the answer to this question out of *self-effort*, the other precondition of successful learning, the sense of achievement is guaranteed.

There is no progress without effort. But effort takes time.
How should an adult, a working person, manage this?

Answer: *One should connect language learning with either work or leisure.* And not at the expense of them but to supplement them.

What does this apparent circle-squaring mean?

Let's take work first. A fair part of a person's work today is self-improvement, supplementing one's knowledge. A foreign language can be very important in expanding the specialized knowledge of an engineer, a remedial teacher, a skilled worker, a music instructor, a physician, a foreign trader, etc.

What a learner must realize is that his own need of a language may be equally specialized; that is, he doesn't need the whole language.

When I set out to learn Japanese in 1956, there was no teacher and no course book to be found in Hungary.

My motivation for learning Japanese was to translate a chemical patent, a job that I had heroically (i.e., rashly) taken on. Fortunately, the large number of formulas, figures, captions, and charts helped me in solving this hopeless-looking task.

First I had to determine, based on the text in my hands, what kind of language Japanese was: if it agglutinates (uses suffixes) like Hungarian does, if it inflects (bends words) like German does, or if it isolates, like English and Chinese do.

Although I managed to get hold of a dictionary, it was not a technical one. In any case, those who have read technical/scientific texts know that they (not dictionaries) are the richest—and, unfortunately, the only reliable—source of technical terms.

Technical *knowledge* is worth more than the best dictionary in translating technical documents. If, for example, there is an acid and a base standing on one side of an equation of a chemical process, a chemist will not have to rack his or her brain: he or she will know that the words (or hieroglyphs) on the other end of the equals sign mean salt plus water.

My experience with Japanese was an extreme case. I admit that not everyone has the patience or time for research like that. (The translation, in fact, went creeping at a snail's pace at the beginning, but I got the hang of it after a week and was earning 20 or 30 forints for each day's work.) But the rule holds that for every language, student, and level, technical knowledge is often the key that opens the gate of language learning.

Whenever I am asked how I was able to succeed in many languages in a relatively short period of time, I always make a bow in spirit to the source of all knowledge: books. My advice to learners can thus be expressed in one word: read!

It cannot be denied, though, that a personal exchange of views—a live conversation—will often leave a more lasting mark in our memory than what is in books.

In practice, however, relationships are not easy to establish and not easy to maintain. Apart from your teachers, who can you expect to be at your disposal and to endure your stuttering attempts with resignation (or maybe even correct them)? Can you expect your foreign acquaintances to always be patient—especially if you can already communicate with them in a common language?

Apart from a conversation with oneself, which I keep advocating so frequently (and which I named *autologue* because neither *monologue* nor *dialogue* covers the concept), there is one situation I find suitable for conversation: a foreign relative, friend, or acquaintance visiting you who—out of gratitude for showing him around—will allow you to practice with him. He might even warn you—possibly tactfully—of your mistakes.

By the way, it is not only an individual but also a national trait that determines how much someone tolerates the incorrect, broken speech of non-natives. A phlegmatic Englishman will not bother in the least. He has gotten used to the fact that even his compatriots speak differently, depending on their residence and social class, let alone speakers of American and Canadian English and the "faulty" pronunciation of job seekers who arrive from the former British colonies.

French people are characterized by a nationwide intolerance. If one is good-mannered, they will only grumble to themselves; if one is uneducated, they will express their dislike with a grimace. I think it is their pride that makes them aggressive. They haven't yet gotten used to the fact that French, once a means of communication between emperors and ambassadors, is now stumbling from the lips of low-budget tourists.

I see another difficulty in practicing a language with others. An uninteresting partner is uninteresting in a foreign language as well.

I have written about how much I suffered in Japan because everyone wanted to practice their English with me and I couldn't attain with the greatest effort to get answers in Japanese to my questions asked in Japanese. In the end, someone took pity on me and recommended a certain Mr. Matsumoto, who understood my sorrow and showed willingness to converse with me in Japanese in the afternoons.

Mr. Matsumoto proved to be a Buddhist monk. He was indeed ready to talk in Japanese, but unfortunately his only topic was Buddhism; specifically, that 11 of its 12 branches held completely false views. Only the branch that he followed was the true one. While he was explaining to me what the sole correct interpretation of the Lotus Sutra was for the third hour, I slipped away.

7

Let's Read!

≈

THE DISCOVERY that books are the utmost means of retaining and obtaining knowledge was made by numerous people before me. What I would like to add to this well-known fact are only two points: first, that you should dare to include reading in your learning program at the very beginning, and second, that you should read *actively*. You need to meet linguistic phenomena frequently so that you can find a way through a language's twists and turns.

I have said numerous times on radio and TV that books, which can be consulted at any time, questioned again and again, and read into scraps, cannot be rivaled as a language-learning tool.

In one of his short stories Dezső Kosztolányi[37] beautifully describes learning a language from a book. Some excerpts are worth inserting here.

> That summer, my only thought was having a rest, playing ball, and swimming. Therefore, I didn't bring along anything to work with. At the last minute, I threw a Portuguese book into my baggage.
>
> …in the open, by necessity, I resigned myself

---

37. Hungarian writer and poet of the early 20th century.

to the book, and in the prison of my solitude, formed by dolomite rocks on one side and vast forests on the other, between the sky and the water, I started to make the text out. At first it was difficult. Then I got the hang of it. I resolved I would still get to the bottom of it, without a master or a dictionary. To spur my instinct and creativity, I imagined I would be hit by some great trouble were I not to understand it exactly, or maybe an unknown tyrant would even condemn me to death.

It was a strange game. The first week, I sweated blood. The second, I intuited what the book was about. The third week, I greeted the birds in Portuguese, who then chatted with me...

...I doubt if I could ever use Portuguese in my life or if I would be able to read any other Portuguese books. But it is not important. I did not regret this summer's steeplechase. I wonder about those who learn a language for practical reasons rather than for itself. It is boring to know. The only thing of interest is learning.

...An exciting game, a coquettish hide-and-seek, a magnificent flirt with the spirit of humanity. Never do we read so fluently and with such keen eyes as in a hardly known, new language. We grow young by it, we become children, babbling babies, and we seem to start a new life. This is the elixir of my life.

...Sometimes I think of it with a certain joy that I can even learn Chinese at my ancient age and that I can recall the bygone pleasure of childhood when I first uttered in the superstitious, old language "mother," and I fall asleep with this word: "milk."[38]

---

38. Excerpts from the short story "Portugálul olvasok" [I read in Portuguese], in *Erős várunk, a nyelv* [Our strong fortress, language].

After this testimony of lyrical beauty, let me say that although more efficient means of learning exist, more accessible and obliging ones do not. In order to have an hour's dialogue with a book, the most you need to do is amble to the nearest library. If it were as easy to get hold of an intelli- gent, cordial, and patient partner, I would recommend that instead.

I mention the library only as a last resort. I recommend buying your own books for language learning. They can be spiced with underlines, question marks, and exclamation points; they can be thumbed and dog-eared, plucked to their essential core, and annotated so that they become a mirror of yourself.

What shall you write in the margins? Only the forms and phrases you have understood and figured out from the context.

Ignore what you can't immediately understand. If a word is important, it will occur several times and explain itself anyway. Base your progress on the known, not the unknown. The more you read, the more phrases you will write in the margins. The knowledge you obtain will be much deeper than what you will derive from the dictionary. The sense of achievement provides you with an emotional-affective charge: You have sprung open a lock; you have solved a little puzzle.

I would like to emphasize once again that my method is designed to supplement and accelerate teacher-guided learning rather than replace it.

There is an old joke about coffees in Budapest that applies here:

> Coffees in Budapest have an advantage—
>   they have no coffee substitute
> They have a disadvantage—
>   they have no coffee bean

And they have a mystery—
what makes them black?

You can discover these elements in teacher-guided learning as well.

Its unquestioned advantage: the reliability of the linguistic information and the regularity of the lessons. [School is what it says it is, for better or worse.]

Its disadvantage: inconvenience, an often-slow pace, and less opportunity for selective learning. [School is often not conducive to real learning.]

In the end, the classic, teacher-guided method has its own mystery. [What makes school "school"?]

It is usually difficult to find a teacher who suits your disposition. It involves luck, just like marriage or any other relationship with adults. The same lesson that bores the lively student may intimidate the student used to slower work.

But even if you manage to find a teacher whose temperament suits yours, it is not always easy to attend classes regularly with the pace of life today. In big cities a lot of time is consumed by commuting, especially after 5:00 p.m. This is the time when one would generally be going to class.

It is a special complication that it is not always pedagogically sound, not to mention financially difficult, to take lessons *alone* for years. Besides the great financial expenditure, this kind of learning is disadvantageous because it is difficult to sustain one's attention for the 60 minutes of the typical lesson. On the other hand, if you study with others, you will likely find partners who are so advanced that they will run you over, or others who are so weak that they will hold you back. In classes, the more lively and uninhibited ones will "suck away the air" from those with a more passive nature, despite all the efforts of the teacher. It is also a special danger in large groups that you will hear your fellow students' bad pronunciation more than your teacher's perfected speech.

Learning in threes promises the best results because some kind of competition, which incites endeavor, tends to develop between the partners. Also, the informality of the threesome means you can learn in a relaxed way without the tenseness and artificiality of the typical foreign language class.

To return to the well-known black coffee joke, the classic, teacher-guided method has its own mystery. The question is how to supplement it with personal methods. I will deal with the most important of these, reading, in the next chapter.

8

Why and What
We Should Read

≈

WE DON'T expect intellectual endeavor to build character anymore. (The bulk of today's language students are past the age of character development anyway.) But if you approach a language as an intellectual sport, a leisure activity comparable to crossword puzzle solving (i.e., an assessment and verification of your abilities), you may set about the work without dislike.

We should read because it is books that provide knowledge in the most interesting way, and it is a fundamental truth of human nature to seek the pleasant and avoid the unpleasant. The traditional way of learning a language (cramming 20–30 words a day and digesting the grammar supplied by a teacher or course book) may satisfy at most one's sense of duty, but it can hardly serve as a source of joy. Nor will it likely be successful.

Man lernt Grammatik aus der Sprache, nicht Sprache aus der Grammatik (One learns grammar from language, not language from grammar)—this truth was stated at the end of the 19th century. Coming at the time when dead languages were studied via grammar translation, this slogan by Toussaint and Langenscheidt was received as revolutionary. It is, however, clear today that the most reliable carriers of language—ordinary books—are at the same time course books as well. The only thing to be added to the above slogan is that books don't only teach grammar but also provide the most painless means of obtaining vocabulary.

There is a separate chapter on vocabulary in this book, but the importance of the question deserves touching on here. The automatic-mechanical memory of our childhood is gone, and the logic of our adult mind is of little help. But in order to be able to express our thoughts and understand others', we need thousands of phrases.

How many? Without delving into the extensive literature on what an average vocabulary is, I propose one approximate number here. Our Hungarian pocket dictionaries usually contain 20–30,000 basic terms (entries). At the level that I call *B* in a later chapter, we use approximately 50–60% of this vocabulary.

Let me ask whoever has reached this stage a question: what percentage of this respectable vocabulary did you obtain "legally," that is, by looking up their meanings in a dictionary or having their meanings explained? I suspect not many. You came by the bulk of your understanding without lifting a finger, by a more comfortable means than dictionaries, course books, or teachers: books.

Learning grammar doesn't try the adult mind as much as vocabulary acquisition. Aversion to grammar is still a universal feature of the technologically minded youth of our time, however. Yet without knowledge of grammar, one cannot fully learn to write.

The human mind is characterized by the fact that the question of "why?" pops up immediately in connection with any new kind of phenomenon. In languages, it is rules that give the reason. Ignoring them would be such a sin as ignoring the laws of chemistry, genetics, or crystallography.

We cannot take the stance that one of the first Russian teachers took after the liberation. This brave amateur—let's call him Eksiy—immigrated to Hungary in the 1920s. Those interested in Russian put him to use in the spring of 1945 and learned from him that "boy" was *мальчик* (*mal'chik*) and "girl" was *девочка* (*devochka*). But when they asked him why one became *мальчика* (*mal'chik***a**) and the other *девочку* (*devochk***u**) in the accusative, he racked his brain for a while and then just shrugged his shoulders and said: "My God, it's nothing but a sort of Russianism."

A learned mind is not content with the automatic acquisition of language facts. It looks for reasons, just as it does in other disciplines. The question is what *medium* we should use to navigate through the tangles of a foreign grammar.

Several decades ago we would have received an unambiguous answer to this question: Latin. Obligatory Latin instruction primes the mind for foreign language learning.

Sadly, those who are busy eradicating international phrases from Hungarian (and looking for more or less affected words to replace them) fail to recognize this. Maybe they just have the desire to draw their swords if someone says *konnektor* instead of *dugaszolóaljzat*.[39]

The imposing cathedral of a language cannot be built without grammar or vocabulary. What we dislike about grammar is that it is often taught without regard for usefulness, for its own sake.

Grammar should be second nature to the learner

When you stop at a red light at an intersection, this action is not preceded by a complicated train of thought (if I don't obey the red light, I will cause confusion in traffic, I may be fined, I may get into mortal danger, etc.). Your reflexes have been established and you obey them. The habit was born, and the proper behavior is now automatic (keeping in mind that exceptions can and do exist).

---

39. Both mean power outlet in Hungarian. The second literally means plugging socket and is a form that is rarely used.

This pattern-of-behavior paradigm is well known and goes by different terms. Psychology calls it a "dynamic stereotype"; English linguistics simply calls it a "pattern." I would call it a "last" to be clear and colloquial.

How do we make a question from a Hungarian statement? Simply by changing the intonation of the sentence: "*Beszél angolul*" → "*Beszél angolul?*"

If one speaks English, such an important change in meaning is entrusted to special auxiliaries.

"He speaks English" → "Does he speak English?"

The "last" develops from a conscious principle. Once it is made, you can use it for emerging new forms.

Those who don't like the analogy of a last may think of the more poetic "tuning fork." I dare to state that whenever you open your mouth to speak a foreign word, this is what you rely on: you strike it in your "mind's ear" and you listen: unless it rings false, you will start speaking.

Learning a language consists of internalizing patterns (whether you call them lasts or tuning forks)

The language-learning method that is good is the one that enables you to learn the most reliable patterns relatively quickly. The precondition of internalizing them is to face the correct forms as much as possible until they become automatic.

For both purposes—elaboration and frequent repetition—books are the best means. Let's read!

A book can be pocketed and discarded, scrawled and torn into pages, lost and bought again. It can be dragged out from a suitcase, opened in front of you when having a snack, revived at the moment of waking, and skimmed through once again before falling asleep. It needs no notice by phone if you can't attend the appointment written in the calendar. It won't get mad if awakened from its slumber during your sleepless nights. Its message can be swallowed whole or chewed into tiny pieces. Its content lures you for intellectual adventures and it satisfies your spirit of adventure. You can get bored of it—but it won't ever get bored of you.

Books are eternal companions. When you grow out of one you simply discard it for another.

A book is the simplest and most easily accessible—even if not necessarily the most efficient—means of creating a personal linguistic microclimate.

I haven't yet encountered the term linguistic microclimate in the scholarly literature, but it is such a self-evident concept that it certainly wasn't invented by me. As opposed to macroclimate—like the language of the country you live in—I mean the linguistic environment that immediately surrounds you in your studies and which you can, to an extent, create for yourself, even in your home. This is the small linguistic realm nurses and nannies once managed to create around the children under their care, in Hungarian counts' castles and children's nurseries. Today we have a more democratic means for this purpose: books and someone you have to learn how to tolerate even on your glummest days—your own self.

This is why I am such an enthusiastic fan of monologues. If I talk with myself, I am relieved that my partner will not be indignant at long hesitations, grammatical agreements difficult to manage, and vocabulary gaps completed in the mother tongue. All I suggest is that monologues be silent. This is to avoid learning bad pronunciation from yourself and to prevent passersby from thinking that your tongue has been loosened by alcohol.

With some willpower, you can develop the habit of discussing your experiences with yourself in a foreign language. Again, it is only a matter of self-discipline.

Not so long ago, I spent a couple of weeks in Andalusia. I was alone. I sought others, but found hardly any connection with the locals (though, in truth, I was also afraid of my pronunciation being corrupted by the ugly dialect spoken there). Therefore, Spanish was represented to me only in advertisements, signboards, book titles in shop windows, and speeches in churches and cinemas. In this void I managed to accustom myself to silent monologizing in Spanish to such a degree that on the way back home, it took the greatest effort to switch over to English, which I was supposed to use at a conference starting the next day.

The fact that a linguistic microclimate is more important than a linguistic macroclimate is proven by many of our older émigré compatriots. No matter where they live, they can't acquire the foreign language properly even after 10–15 years' residence, simply because they have built a Hungarian wall around themselves and their children, bridge partners, or even business partners.

And how many sad examples we know concerning the opposite situation! Indeed, how can we maintain our knowledge of our native language without saying a word in it for years? I believe it can only be done through inner monologues, and therefore I wholeheartedly endorse this practice for my fellow language learners.

I cannot cite a more beautiful example of linguistic loyalty in a foreign macroclimate than that of Alexander Lenard.[40] He left Hungary at the age of eight. And though he lived in remote regions of Brazil for decades, where our language probably wasn't even heard of, he wrote his great books with a mastery of Hungarian comparable to the beautiful style of Ferenc Móra.[41] I never asked him but it is my conviction that his reading in Hungarian was complemented by subconscious inner monologues to a degree that he could have been a teacher of writing.

Returning to books, the question arises: what shall we read? Answer: A text that is of interest to you. *Interesse ist*

---

40. Born Lénárd Sándor (1910–1972); Hungarian writer, poet, translator, physician, and musician. He lived in Brazil from 1951 till his death.
41. Hungarian writer of the early 20th century, best known for his children's novel *The Treasure-Hunting Coat*.

stärker als Liebe as they put it in German. (Interest[edness] is stronger than love.) And interest beats the fiercest enemy: boredom.

We must admit that in a foreign language in which we have a deficient vocabulary, reading can be boring. After five, 10, or 20 minutes, we may get the feeling of coming to a linguistic deadlock if we're not motivated to continue. We need something more to help us get through it.

That something is the *pull* of a truly interesting text.

What someone finds interesting is a matter of age, intellectual level, trade, and hobby. I took the trouble of asking 10 people I knew who had followed my method and asked them what had helped them through their linguistic deadlocks (if any). I include their answers here in the order and form I received them.

P. S., pensioner: "Catalogs...so I can arrange my stamps."

Ö. M., high school student, reader of sports' pages: "It's uncool when you don't know what matches foreign soccer teams are preparing for."

B. N., typewriter repairman, reader of technical manuals: "You know, I invent technical devices; that's what I need it for."

K. V., hairdresser: "I read everything about Gregory Peck and the other stars."

P. F., grandmother: "Well, I never, how much they dare to write down in today's romance novels!"

A. M., department head, Federal Ministry: "I love detective stories. I can't stop before I learn who the murderer was!"

J. L., printer: "I wanted to learn the lyrics of the tunes I was whistling."

I. M., haberdashery assistant: "It began with Princess Diana. I actually specialized in her..."

S. W., first-year medic, reader of medical texts: "I'd like to do neurophysiology."

M. R., window dresser, reader of fashion magazines: "You just keep looking at those gorgeous clothes in the fashion mags and you can't understand what's written under them."

Many of my adult male acquaintances were helped through their deadlocks by their interest in politics. Reading between the lines is a typical Hungarian trait. I think the ink (sorry, the blood) hadn't yet dried on the Etelköz contract[42] when our ancestors put their heads together and said, "Yes, all right, but what is between the lines?"

The more our curiosity is satisfied by reading, the less we need discipline to get through our deadlocks.

You didn't put your bicycle back against the wall after your first fall, nor did you chop up your skis when you fell into the snow—despite the fact that these memories were preserved by painful bruises. You held on because you knew that your trials would be less and less and the joys provided by the new skill would be greater and greater. (Even though these were not even about a new world, whose gates are opened by a little persistence.)

Speaking skill is developed most by reading today's plays and colorful modern short stories and novels that have a good pace. "Situational elements," as they call them, are built into the background of the story so they steal into your memory along with the background. This will be the context with which they will emerge when you get into the same situation as described.

The advantage of "situational" texts is that they provide usable vocabulary and sentence patterns. Their disadvantage is that they are fairly difficult to understand.

---

42. A blood contract is said to have been made between the seven leaders of the early Hungarians in the 9th century in Etelköz, an area thought to be in today's south Ukraine or south Russia. Later the tribes settled in the Carpathian Basin, which includes present-day Hungary.

Those venturing to learn a foreign language should be prepared to learn to understand not one but at least two forms of it: the written and the spoken. The average language learner who has chosen my method will cope with the former more easily than the latter.

Books have descriptive parts. In these, writers quote themselves and since they are good stylists by profession, they roll out nice, regularly formed sentences in front of you. Also, teachers are educators because they are supposed to speak in a clever and precise way. Unfortunately, all this has nothing—or not always has anything—to do with actual situations in life.

Why don't you try noticing, my dear fellow language learners, what your native language sounds like? You omit letters, clip endings, and glide over words. G. B. Shaw once said that he spoke English in three different languages: one in his plays, one in his day-to-day life, and one in his intimate relationships. This stratification, which exists in all languages, is the most striking in English, because English is at the intersection of two big language groups: Germanic and Romance. Accordingly, it has a large number of Norman (French) and Anglo-Saxon terms.

It is a frequently cited fact that English has two sets of words for farm animals and their corresponding meats. The living animals are expressed with words of Germanic origin—calf (German *Kalb*), swine (G. *Schwein*) and ox (G. *Ochse*)—because the servants who guarded them were the conquered Anglo-Saxons. The names of the meats are of Romance origin—veal (French *veau*), pork (F. *porc*) and beef (F. *bœuf*)—because those who enjoyed them were the conquering Norman masters.

It is commonly known that foreigners are easier to understand if they are educated. However, an acquaintance of mine, who was in London and who spoke good German and no French, was surprised to experience that the case was just the opposite there: she was able to follow the information by the policeman on the corner much better than the speech of her erudite colleagues. For the sake of language learning, she even visited some churches and listened to sermons. (I wouldn't ever miss this old trick; you can study the language and rest your sightseeing-blistered feet at the same time.)[43] Well, this friend was despairing because she didn't understand a single word from the sermons she heard in London.

Out of curiosity, she brought home the texts of the sermons handed out after services. We examined them a bit and saw that the priest almost always favored words of Norman origin. We had good fun retranslating the English text by replacing every Norman word with its Germanic equivalent (e.g., "commence" with "begin").

Stratification is less palpable in descriptive words that depict the background of the action. This language is much more homogeneous. It doesn't show, for example, the differences required by various levels of politeness in spoken language. It is a refreshing achievement of our age that the usage of over-polite expressions, such as "dearest," "taking the liberty" (of doing something), or "having the honor" (to do something), is decreasing. (On the other hand, it is regrettable that we begin to use less of *Tessék!*[44] It is a pity because if you consider its original meaning, you should find it kind from the viewpoint of the psychology of language. The only nicer way of offering the thirsty traveler a glass of wine may be the one in Transylvania: *Szeresse!*[45])

For a valuable "dictionary" of spoken language, you can use today's plays or the dialogues of novels. Classical works are not suitable for this purpose. I asked my young German

---

43. This book was written during the era of Hungarian socialism, in which religion was frowned upon. Therefore going to a church often required an excuse (e.g., a rest).
44. "Here you are" (like when handing sth). It literally means "may it please you!" but this meaning is far from obvious for native speakers.
45. "May you love it!"

friend who was raised on Jókai[46] how she liked her new roommate. *"Délceg, de kevély,"*[47] she replied.

Why do some words become comical in a couple of decades while others remain unchanged? We don't know and we also don't know why we accepted some words from the age of the Language Reform[48] and why we rejected others. We use *zongora*[49] and *iroda*[50] without any kind of aversion but we don't even know anymore for what purpose *tetszice*[51] and *gondolygász*[52] were proposed. *Kórtan,*[53] put forward by Pál Bugát, became a full-fledged word, but *éptan*[54] didn't; out of Bugát's innovations, we accepted *rekeszizom*[55] instead of *diafragma* but we don't use *gerj*[56] and we rejected *fogondzat*[57] for *magzat.*[58] *Habent sua fata verba*—words, too, have their own destiny.

Course books and even today's popular phrase books are often written in stilted language and thus are not reliable sources of live speech compared to a modern literary work. I leafed through a travel dictionary recently (it wasn't

---

46. Mór Jókai: prolific Hungarian writer of the 19th century.

47. "Stately but haughty," expressed in a lofty and old-fashioned way.

48. A movement of the late 18th and early 19th century when approximately 10,000 Hungarian words were coined (most of which are still in use), providing the language with the vocabulary necessary to keep up with the developments of the age and enabling it to become the official language of the country.

49. piano, coined from *zeng* (resound).

50. office, coined from *ír* (write).

51. aesthetics, coined from *tetszik* (it pleases). Today it is *esztétika.*

52. philosopher, coined from *gondol(kodik)* (think) and *-ász* (occupation suffix). Today it is *filozófus* or *bölcselő.*

53. pathology, still in use today.

54. hygienics, from *ép* (healthy, sound) and *tan* (study, cf. -ology). Today it is *egészségtan* (lit., health study).

55. diaphragm, still in use today.

56. stirring (n), from *gerjed* (be stirred). Today it is *indulat.*

57. embryo, coined from *fogan* (be conceived).

58. embryo, from the 13th century; related to *mag* (core, seed), still in use today.

published in Hungary) and I couldn't help laughing when I imagined the dialogue recommended for learning in the context of today's life: "I would like to get acquainted with the places of historical interest and the important agricultural products of your country."

It is much more likely that a conversation between a native and a non-native will sound something like this:

"Hey, how 'bout getting a cup of joe around here?"

"Oh, slower please, I don't understand. Getting what?"

"A cup of joe!"

"What is it? A cup of coffee?"

"Of course!"

"Sorry, I can't, I have to go back to the…uh, what do you call it?"

"To the hotel? Well, see you!"

I admit that a course book cannot teach and an instructor cannot recommend using the words "hey," "oh," "well," "y'know," "huh," "kind of" and the like. However, they occur much more frequently in everyday chats than well-bred "dictionary words." So I return to my soapbox: until you naturally begin to acquire such words through usage, you can learn such colloquialisms from today's prose in the most painless way.

9

How We Should Read

≈

AT FIRST, we should read with a blitheness bordering on superficiality; later on, with a conscientiousness close to distrust.

It is especially my male and technically minded fellow students whom I would like to persuade to do this.

I frequently see men reading the easiest pulp fiction, armed with heavy dictionaries. They will read one word in the book and then look it up in the dictionary. No wonder they soon get bored of reading and end up sighing with relief when it is time for the news so they can turn on the TV.

Conscientiousness is a nice virtue, but at the beginning of language learning, it is more of a brake than an engine. It is not worth looking up every word in the dictionary. It is much more of a problem if a book becomes flavorless in your hands because of interruptions rather than not knowing whether the inspector watches the murderer from behind a blackthorn or a hawthorn.

If a word is important, it will come up again, and its meaning will become apparent from the context. This kind of vocabulary acquisition, which requires some thinking, leaves a much more lasting impression than reaching for the dictionary and acknowledging the meaning of the word absent-mindedly. If you reach understanding at the expense of brainwork, it was *you* who contributed to creating the connection and *you* who found the solution. This joy is like the one felt completing a crossword puzzle.

The sense of achievement sweetens the joy of work and makes up for the boredom of effort. It incorporates the most interesting thing in the world even into an indifferent text. You wonder what it is? *Our own selves.*

It was *me myself* who gleaned the word and *me myself* who deciphered the meaning of the sentence. It deserves some subconscious self-recognition, a secret little self-congratulation. You are compensated for your invested work, and you have the motivation for further activity right away.

It is proven by experience that initial dynamism is a good way to start reading in a foreign language, since a habit can be made of it like every other human activity. The main thing is to *not get discouraged* by the unfriendly medium of the foreign language text.

Who hasn't felt a mild shiver when throwing oneself into the cool waters of a lake? Who hasn't desired to climb back to the sunlit sand? And who hasn't been happy after a minute or two, after getting used to the cold of the water, for resisting the temptation? An *interesting* foreign language text should help the "swimmer" over the initial aversion and discouragement of reading.

But if the engine is running properly, one has to learn how to brake as well. When you've worked through a text and put the book down with the uplifting feeling that you've understood what it is about, literature should become the raw material of learning.

To my knowledge, aside from Kosztolányi's story "I Read in Portuguese," there is only one other work in Hungarian literature that deals with language learning: a charming tale by Mikszáth called "Aussi Brebis." The main character in the story hires a French tutor for his sons. The teenagers want to evade this girl (and learning) at all costs, so they invent the excuse that she doesn't speak French. They have their father promise to let them stop learning once they manage to catch her ignorant. In order to expose her, they keep browsing the dictionary and the grammar book until they acquire the language themselves without noticing it.

Let's be sly and suspicious ourselves, too, in this second stage. Let's regard words and sentences as touchstones to see if the writer breaks any rules.

I can predict the result. It will turn out that André Maurois speaks better French than you, Vera Panova better Russian, and Taylor Caldwell better English. In this fight, you cannot *prevail* but you can *win*. Your knowledge develops and becomes consolidated. By the way, I didn't mention these three specific authors by chance. Their fluent, natural style makes them suitable for warming up to a language.

To those who don't dare to embark on original, unabridged literary works, I can recommend adapted texts with all my heart. The classics of world literature have been rewritten, for language-learning purposes, into simpler sentences with a reduced vocabulary. They are available in every bookstore, and they can be borrowed from libraries for free, but I don't recommend the latter. Course books are for scrawling. When they have fallen apart by too much use, they can be bought again.

Language is present in a piece of writing like the sea in a single drop. If you have the patience to turn the text up and down and inside out, break it into pieces and put it together again, and shake it up and let it settle again—then you can learn remarkably much from it.

Lajos Kossuth,[59] whose orations are given as models in 20th-century English rhetoric books, learned English in an Austrian prison. He used 16 lines of a Shakespeare play as a starting point. "I literally had to surmise English grammar from them. And once I had and perfectly understood the 16 lines, I knew enough English so that I only had to enrich my vocabulary."

---

59. Hungarian politician and freedom fighter of the 19th century.

10

Reading and Pronunciation

≈

LANGUAGE KNOWLEDGE consists of understanding others and making yourself understood. The aim of language learning is to acquire these two abilities in both listening/speaking and reading/writing.

Conceiving the meaning of texts and speech is an analytical process. *Communicating* a message in speech or in writing is a synthetic activity.

If you neglect either of these skills, you have only accomplished part of your goal. In practice, however, shortshrifting one or the other occurs. It is usually not for matters of principle but for lack of time.

Listening/speaking and reading/writing are interconnected and they enhance each other, but it is proven by experience that less than complete mastery of them can still be useful. I met a hotel receptionist in Rome who negotiated in seven languages with perfect pronunciation (even in Hungarian) but couldn't write properly in any of them (not even in Italian). On the other hand, Arany and Petőfi,[60] who presented us with eternal values of translation, had no idea of pronunciation. For example, the rhythm of "The Bards of Wales" by Arany demands that "lord mayor" be read as "lord ma-yohr."

---

60. János Arany and Sándor Petőfi: 19th-century Hungarian poets.

Books, alas, cannot teach you exact pronunciation. I was an ear-witness of a nice episode at the London airport a couple of years ago. The immigration officer was thumbing the passport of an Indian student. "Purpose of trip: studies," he read aloud. "And what will be the subject of the studies?" he inquired. "Luv," the student replied, who must have never heard how the word "law" is pronounced.

The officer, with his English composure, didn't even bat an eyelid. He let the passenger pass his checkpoint and only murmured to himself that "love is more or less the same around the world; it really isn't worth flying thousands of miles to study what little differences there are."

Pronunciation is one of the most difficult tasks of language learning and one of the most important touchstones of your language mastery. Although it isn't worth very much without a fair knowledge of vocabulary and grammar, this is what your knowledge is judged by when you first speak. It plays approximately the same role in representing your skills as looks do for women. A pretty woman will definitely be *right* at the moment she appears. Later on, she may turn out to be stupid, boring, or even malicious, but she has won the first battle anyway.

Teaching pronunciation has a shorter history than that of grammar or vocabulary. It has only become really important since the teaching of *living* languages started. But this short time proved to be enough for several delusions to circulate. Let's take them one by one.

Good pronunciation needs an ear. Even if it is necessary, it is not the one commonly meant (that is, for music). I have a host of outstanding Hungarian musicians as witnesses, who speak foreign languages fluently and with a rich vocabulary, but with a distinctive Hungarian accent. I would rather call the necessary skill "auditive intuition"—perceiving the sounds different from your mother tongue and being able to differentiate them in your brain.

It is another delusion that *in order to learn good pronun-*

ciation, it is enough to hear it. You might as well suppose that by diligently watching world champion figure skaters on TV you will be able to do the triple loop or the double axel jump on the ice rink the next day.

Champions and their trainers approach perfection step by step, with never-ceasing, self-devoting work that extends to a thousand details. I know that the average language learner has no intention of entering the olympiad of languages. But whoever learns to sing finds it natural that they have to practice scales—for long hours and for long years. The way to good pronunciation also requires practicing scales, but here it is called a drill.

An infant's babble is heavenly music only for his or her parents; it is diligent scales for the baby. Babies keep trying to create the sounds that flow towards them from their environment. Unlike their grown-up fellow language students, however, they have two advantages: they don't have to forget another set of sounds during this activity, and they don't start out from *letters,* which an adult reacts to with *ingrained sounds.*

There was an elementary school in Buda[61] where French was taught from the first grade on. My little son attended it, and I took part in one of the classes. Each child pronounced *quatre* so perfectly (like "cut") that I heaved a deep sigh of envy. A sympathetic fellow mother said to me from behind, "The reason why they don't say it 'cut-r' is because they have no idea the letter 'r' is in the word."

Can we draw a conclusion from this that you should first *hear* a word and then *see* it only afterwards? I am afraid not. Not for theoretical reasons but for practical ones. You couldn't set your learning process to such a long-term method of obtaining vocabulary even if you supposed it was enough to hear the pronunciation of a word only once or twice and you wouldn't ever make a mistake again. This is

---

61. The western, hilly part of Budapest.

because public enemy number one of language students is forgetting.

You should fight forgetting with repetition. The precondition of repetition is that the phrases to be memorized should be commonly used by speakers of the language. However, this cannot always be ensured even in the very center of a foreign-language environment, let alone thousands of miles away from it.

I have written it several times but I must emphasize it once again (and I dare not promise it will be the last time): it is only books that provide an unlimited amount of repetition. It is only reading that can be returned to again and again without being an ordeal. And a book is expected to bear witness: it lets itself be interrogated again and again, with an invariable readiness. Besides its million assets, it is only culpable in one thing: it cannot speak. Or rather, it does speak to you, but in accordance with your mother tongue pronunciation habits. There is nothing to be done: you have to learn the foreign language pronunciation rules, and not in general but *by consciously comparing them with your mother tongue*—by contrasting them.

It is essential even for those who have an ear for languages, that is, those who approach a new language with his or her *ears*. And it is essential for those who have unlimited access to audio laboratories.

Some people will learn how to pronounce the English word "film" by their auditive intuition. But it is a more certain method if you make it conscious that there is no short "i" in English: once it is short, it immediately shifts towards "e."[62] It is the job of a good teacher—or, if lacking, radio, cassettes, or CDs—to direct one's attention to this and similar rules.

---

62. Compare "sit" and "seat": the former is not only shorter but also more open. What an English speaker would have to learn in turn is that the short vowel in Hungarian retains the closed quality of the long one.

This is, however, only part of the lesson, and not even its more difficult part. It is at least as important to be able to *reproduce* the sound, stress, intonation, and rhythm of speech that you have made conscious. This is where men, "the crowns of Creation," are handicapped compared to women. Imitation ability is much less common in men, who tend to be too shy to venture a facial expression alien to them.

When someone resolves to acquire it, he will have to diligently practice "scales" on the sounds and sound clusters unknown in his mother tongue. You wonder which ones? First of all, those whose *incorrect pronunciation changes the meaning of the word.*

A Hungarian knows several versions of the sound "e." Therefore he will not have a problem comprehending words with "e" that are pronounced differently. However, the Englishman is not so fortunate. The English word "bed" pronounced with a closed "e" and the word "bad" pronounced with an open "e" mean completely different things. "Bed manners," mentioned so frequently in the literature of our age, should not be confused with "bad manners."

I would like to mention two aspects from my own experience. One is that you should do this "phonetic drill" with words that don't exist in the target language: nonsense words. The reason for this is so you don't confuse them with actual words.

For example, the difference between the sounds "w" and "v" is especially difficult for us Hungarians. Let's practice, then, syllables like *wo—vo, wa—va, we—ve, wi—vi*, etc. Walking or taking a bath, waiting for the tram, or doing your hair are good opportunities for it. I can especially recommend the latter because you can easily check your mouth position in the mirror.

It is also instructive to notice the pronunciation mistakes of foreigners who speak your mother tongue. Listen to them with the *consciousness* so important in language learning. "I've actually understood the pronunciation rules of

German from Siegfried Brachfeld's[63] Hungarian," an attentive friend of mine once told me. Whoever heard a speaker of English asking for *thölthöthollthintha*[64] in a store will never forget the rule of aspiration.

Generally, radio, TV, and language CDs provide good models of pronunciation. Of course, they are worth the time only if you pay special attention to them. For example, listen to how an individual sound is different (shorter or longer, closed or more open, sharper or flatter) from the way it lives in your mind. Even if you learn only one sound at a time, you can still build a decent collection of lasts.

It is even more important that you learn the correct intonation of words and sentences. You can effectively ingrain them in your mind by recording radio and TV programs and playing them back repeatedly. The eternal rule holds here as well: you should do this for a short time but with full intensity. Don't sit next to the radio or the tape recorder with your thoughts wandering among yesterday's experiences or tomorrow's hopes.

TV is an excellent way to learn languages because it often shows the face in close-up: at such times, you can hear the sound and you can practically read the right mouth position from the screen. I envy my foreign—e.g., Dutch—fellow language learners: they see undubbed foreign films on TV and therefore have the opportunity to hear the foreign language for one or two hours a day *and* see the transcription in Dutch in the subtitles, should they miss something.

Even if I understand the reason, I greatly regret that original-language audio tracks are so rare on Hungarian TV. We language students are very grateful for them.

---

63. Popular Master of Ceremonies of German birth, who lived and performed in Hungary in the 1970s.

64. *Töltőtolltinta* means fountain pen ink. Hungarian consonants "p," "t," and "k" are pronounced without aspiration (release of a strong burst of air, like a short "h"), which is usually hard for native speakers of English to master.

There is no need to emphasize the usefulness of language courses, especially if they provide the opportunity to listen to a lesson twice. Let's contribute to the success of classroom language learning by not following it with only half our soul and one of our eyes.

I would be happy to write here that the educational achievements of recent years have solved our language-learning problems. Unfortunately reality hasn't proved our rosy hopes right. Most of us come home from work tired; we are more likely to stick to crime movies and westerns than improve our foreign-language speaking skills. As for teenagers, they are thirsty for pop songs, which usually do not provide clear models of spoken language. Videos can enrich our vocabulary and improve our sentence construction skills, but only if we watch them repeatedly. According to my own informal surveys, this is not typical of fans of videos.

11

What Sort of Languages Do People Study?

≈

UNESCO sent out a questionnaire a couple of years ago to find an answer to the above question. After they had collected the responses, they didn't name any languages. They only reported that people tend to study the languages of peoples living at their country borders because these are the languages they are most likely to use.

If that is the rule, Hungary is partly an exception to it. Of the languages that Hungarians acquire, Czech,[65] Serbian, and Romanian are rare. Our linguistic isolation is such that we have to learn languages with a large "radius of action" to obtain a passport to the world. Happy Switzerland: it has embraced three world languages within its borders. Whichever language a Swiss chooses, he or she will have an open door to several million speakers.

Our language is spoken, apart from Hungarians here and abroad, by only a few hundred people motivated to learn it for some kind of personal (emotional) reason, the interesting nature of its linguistics, or to read our literature.

---

65. The Czech Republic is not a neighbor of Hungary, but Czechoslovakia was until the end of 1992, when it dissolved. Czech and Slovak are mutually intelligible languages.

Thus it is all the more curious how often you seem to meet speakers of Hungarian abroad. When a compatriot of ours is waiting at a red light, stamping his feet in anger and swearing with the impatience typical of those in Budapest, someone often looks back with a smile, indicating that Hungarian is actually a world language and one should not relieve one's temper this way in Brussels or in London.

Many years ago, an international youth conference was held in a northern European city. I admit I was not included in the committee as a representative of Hungarian youth but as an interpreter. To arouse interest among the local population, the organizers suggested a procession and asked the participants to appear, if possible, in national costumes. Along with the natives, our little group applauded the Dutch girls in bonnets, the Japanese girls in kimonos, the Polish guys in mantles, and the Scottish guys in kilts, who provided a really attractive sight.

Suddenly, I noticed the ebony black sons of an African nation approaching naked to the waist, their faces painted in colors, with swinging, purple feather headdresses.

The African group arrived beside us and one of them— the leader, judging by his more colorful feathers and his longer spear—caught sight of us.

"Hi, Kate!" he shouted enthusiastically in flawless Hungarian. "Where are the Budapest guys?"

It was T. M., who had spent four years at a Hungarian university and maybe found nothing surprising about the fact that someone who had been born around the Equator could speak impeccable Hungarian.

How does one decide which language to learn? How does one decide which language his child will learn? The answer is usually connected to usability and facileness.

I will discuss usability in the chapter on the future of languages. As far as easiness is concerned, the decision is personal. In Hungary (as in most other countries outside the "big" languages), we have no lack of teachers, course books, dictionaries, or theoretical and practical literature on methodology. Therefore the learner can select the language that suits him best.

You sometimes hear people claim that there are nice and ugly languages, or rich and poor ones.

Italian is usually considered to be the most beautiful by the layman. It is praised for being soft and melodious.

Italian is pleasant to the ear because it builds its words with many vowels and few consonants. German is considered less so. At best it can compete in the olympiad of languages with sentences like *Laue Lüfte wehen lind.* Is this sentence likable because there are several *l*'s in it, or because it spontaneously evokes its translation, which also flows nicely: "Warm breezes are blowing gently"[66]?

Russian is often considered more manly than ingratiating, though the poet Fyodor Sologub found nice-sounding words to praise his darling:

> *Beley liley, alee lala,*
> *Bela byla ty i ala.*[67]

The original sounds more beautiful than my rough-and-ready translation: "You were white and rosy, whiter than a lily, rosier than a ruby."[68]

"The acoustic phenomena of language are hard to distinguish from the influence of meaning," Béla Zolnai wrote (*Nyelv és hangulat* [Language and atmosphere]). The rigid or soft ring of words doesn't only depend on the combination of sounds! You fall into a reverie when hearing the word "violet": what a gentle, kind little flower. The word "violence" clangs angrily in your ears, although its letters are almost the same. The word "Andalusia" tinkles softly, but

---

66. Hungarian: *"Langyos szellők lágyan lengedeznek."*
67. From *Plamennyi krug* [Circle of flame], 1908.
68. "Ruby" is poetic license; "ЛАЛ" (lal) is red spinel.

"vandalism" clangs roughly, even though both words come from the same root. You react to the word *fülbemászó*[69] one way if it means a catchy tune, and another way if it means an ugly earwig.

Czech and Serbian usually earn bad grades in melodiousness. They are condemned by public opinion because of their complex consonant clusters. *Crni vrh* (black peak) is usually quoted from Serbian: it consists almost solely of consonants. The reason why I think Czech doesn't have a pleasant effect on the ears is because it has word-initial stress: i.e., it is always the first syllable of a word that raps your eardrum. This may be the reason why Hungarian is not considered nice either.

"What do you call your darling?" an Italian soldier in World War I asked his Hungarian comrade.

"I call her *galambom* [my dove]," he replied.

"Ding-dong, galambom," the Italian wondered. "But it's a peal of bells, not an endearment!"

Many have attempted to attribute expressive features to sounds. Few did it more poetically than Kosztolányi:

Oh, the l*'s*	*Full of* l,
elegance,	*full of* i,
and the m*'s*	*full of* n,
melody,	*full of* e,
pastoral	*full of creams,*
poesy	*full of dreams,*
pining for	*full of screams,*
Melanie.	*Melanie.*[70]

---

69. Lit., "into-the-ear-crawling" in Hungarian, used as an adjective of music and as a name of an insect.

70. From the poem "Ilona," translated as "Melanie" by P. Zollman. The Hungarian original: "Ó az i / kelleme, / ó az l / dallama, / mint ódon / ballada, / úgy sóhajt, / Ilona. // Csupa l, / csupa i, / csupa o, / csupa a, / csupa tej, / csupa kéj, / csupa jaj, / Ilona."

Much more prosaically, we can also state that *some* sounds occur in words with *certain* meanings with an above-average frequency—for instance, the vowel /ɪ/ (as in "bit") in the meaning "tiny." Let's just consider the Hungarian words *kis, kicsi* (small, little), *pici* (tiny), German *winzig* (tiny), Russian *mizinyets* (little finger), English *little, itsybitsy, teeny-weeny,* French *minime,* Italian *piccolino,* Spanish *chiquito* (little boy), the word *piti* (petty, no-account) in the Hungarian argot, and *bikini,* even smaller than a *mini* (mini skirt), even if it didn't get the name from its size. Do the words *Donner, tonnerre, thunder, гром гремит (grom gremit:* thundering thunder) sound so grim because of the frequent occurrence of "r," or because of their ominous meanings?

The beauty of a language is, therefore, generally judged by its soft, rigid, melodious, or harsh ring. Other aspects, such as the flexibility of derivation, play hardly any role in grading. Were It the case, Russian would certainly be placed on the winner's stand. It would rank first in *plasticity.*

Gold is said to be the most precious metal because a nugget the size of a cent can be hammered into a sheet of considerable size, without losing the slightest bit of gleam or color. Russian is not dissimilar. For example, let's start with the one-syllable word "СТАТЬ":

стать	*stat'*	become
ставить	*stavit'*	put
оставить	*ostavit'*	leave
остановить	*ostanovit'*	stop
приостановить	*priostanovit'*	suspend
приостанавливать	*priostanavlivat'*	cease
приостанавливаться	*priostanavlivat'sya*	be discontinued
приостанавливаемый	*priostanavlivayemyy*	stoppable

A complicated structure? Undoubtedly. But after all, the cathedral of Milan is complicated too, and you still look at it with awe. The C major scale is simple, but it is not especially nice; however, the Jupiter Symphony, built from it, is a wonderful masterpiece.

Language is a servant and a compliant lamb of human-kind. It varies its existing devices so that every idea should be suitable for translation in its entirety. He who is frightened by the number of suffixes in Finno-Ugric languages should think of the infinite variety of combinations of isolated words in English. The meaning of a sentence depends on what building blocks you move about on the chessboard of your thoughts.

For example, the verb "to turn" changes meaning completely when certain adverbs are added to it. These combinations of verbs and adverbs, called phrasal verbs, need to be remembered one by one, as new words. Here are just a few examples:

I turned down	(I rejected)
you turned up	(you appeared)
he turned in	(he went to bed)
we turned over	(we sold)
you turned out	(you produced)
they turned on	(they switched on)

There is a separate chapter in this book about the question of languages being easy or difficult. One general truth, however, needs to be mentioned here.

The language that is usually considered the easiest to learn is Italian. This is so because there are relatively few rules needed to recognize the relationships of sounds and letters, to build them into words, and to create sentences out of them.

12

Language and Vocabulary

≈

YOU OFTEN hear that there are "poor" and "rich" languages. One language may indeed offer more synonyms for a concept than another; I don't know of any exact survey in the field. However, while a language may be rich in words to express a certain concept, it can be surprisingly deficient in words expressing another. Hungarian is no exception.

Our translators like to sigh that they can't render all the shades of meaning within foreign literary works into Hungarian. I admit that we are poor here and there. For example, we have only the word "hang" for the German words *Stimme, Ton,* and *Laut*.[71] The English words "seed," "nucleus," "pip," "core," and "semen" can *always* be rendered with one Hungarian word, *mag*; the words "grain," "kernel," and "stone" can mostly be rendered with it. But what other language can pride itself on the ability to differentiate between *felszabadulás* and *felszabadítás*, and *felhalmozás* and *felhalmozódás*?[72]

---

71. German: voice, tone/note, sound.

72. *Felszabadulás* and *felszabadítás* mean liberation; *felhalmozás* and *felhalmozódás* mean accumulation. They derive from transitive and in-transitive verbs, which are distinguished in Hungarian but which often coincide in English. Hence, their literal meaning is approximately becoming free vs. setting sb/sth free, and becoming accumulated vs. accumulating sth.

German is usually considered the richest language. Yet it doesn't have separate words to express a) a skill that can be acquired and b) an ability that depends on circumstances, unlike French, Russian, and Polish. In those languages *Je sais écrire, умею писать* (*umeyu pisat'*), and *umiem pisać* mean that I can write because I have learned it; *je peux écrire, могу писать* (*mogu pisat'*), and *mogę pisać* mean that there is no external obstacle to my writing (e.g., I have a pen and it is not forbidden, either). The translators' sigh was caused by the difference between the French *pouvoir* and *savoir: Si jeunesse **savait**, si vieillesse **pouvait***—"If the young only *knew*, if the old only *could.*"

English has a separate auxiliary verb to express possibility depending on permission: *may.* This was what provided the answer for G. B. Shaw when a mediocre translator asked him if he could translate one of his works. "You may, but you can't," he replied. Without these auxiliaries, it could only be rendered awkwardly as "You are allowed, but you are not able."

The above lines about the auxiliary *may* have led me to a topic that often comes up nowadays: the special vocabulary of the young. It is criticized by many and praised by many others; I belong to the latter group. Rarely documented, it often proves indispensable. A teacher explained to a German class that the auxiliary *mögen*[73] has no equivalent in Hungarian. "And what about *csípem*[74]?" the students retorted. Indeed, it would have been a pity for such a short, concise, almost imitative word like *cucc*[75] not to have been born.

The unforgettable Klára Szőllősy once noted what

---

73. *Mögen*: to like. Its traditional Hungarian equivalents are *szeret*, which implies a stronger feeling as it can also mean to love, and *kedvel* (to cherish, to like) (dated)

74. *Csíp*, originally to pinch, is now a slang term that means a positive opinion or a moderate degree of liking.

75. Hungarian: stuff, things, belongings.

a headache it had been for her to translate the following sentence from *The Magic Mountain*: "It is a shame that the most pious attraction to the most intense physical desire is expressed with a single word (*die Liebe*)."

The richness of our Hungarian language—the words *szerelem* and *szeretet*[76]—made the excellent translator's job rather difficult.

---

76. Both mean love in English, the first referring to romantic love and the second implying affection.

13

Vocabulary and Context

≈

"MOM, what does 'TB' mean?"

"It depends, son, on what you are reading. It may be 'textbook' or 'thoroughbred.' If you are reading a sports story, it may be 'tennis ball.' In a medical article, it may mean 'tuberculosis.' In a physics text, it may stand for 'turbulence.'"

The above conversation, taken from my own life, illustrates that words—or in this case abbreviations—cannot be removed from their contexts. One can only understand them—and should only learn them—in their contexts.

Context is a Latin word; it means a material woven together or, in a figurative sense, connection and background. It warrants mentioning here because text is always a woven fabric. You can take a word or phrase out of it but such an isolated unit will only represent the whole as much as a snippet of fabric will represent the bolt of cloth it originated from. The threads interweave and strengthen each other; this is how they give the whole its color, form, and stability.

Surely all of you remember a situation when you had to start speaking a language you hadn't used for years. The wheels of the mind creak with difficulty. You shake your head in anger: you knew the words but now you've forgotten them. Even the simplest words don't come to you. When they finally do come to you, however, they are not from your default language (your native tongue). Rather, they are from another foreign language you have studied. You are annoyed and surprised, but then after 10–20 minutes the words and forms from the "right" language start to fall into place. Your partner wonders and you think to yourself with a silent rapture that you may still be a language genius—although it was but the power of words recalling each other that pulled the context into place.

I've racked my brains for a long time about why *name memory* is the weakest point of one's memory. Commonplace or technical terms crop up in your mind at first call even if you don't use them for years, while sometimes you can't recall the names (especially the first names) of your acquaintances, friends, or even your relatives in spite of great effort.

I bring this all up because my advice for preventing such memory lapses is the same as my method for memorizing words. I mean *mnemonics*, which is the art of putting terms into artificial contexts. The word or name to be memorized should never be left floating in the void but should be associated with another, already-known term or concept. This can be done lexically, semantically, or phonetically, among other ways. For example, I will never forget how a poor man is expressed in Japanese, or a little boy in Italian: both of them sound like "bimbo."[77]

Of course, formal associations are not completely without danger. Richard Katz notes in one of his books that he remembered the Japanese equivalent of "thank you" (*arrigato*) by thinking of the alligator. This must be why he once said to a kind little geisha who helped him with his coat, "Crocodile!"

Not only can a word serve as context, but everything that accompanies it can too, such as facial expressions, intonations, and gestures. That is why we can understand a live, gesticulating speaker more easily than an invisible radio

---

77. *Bimbó* means bud in Hungarian.

announcer, no matter how perfect his or her pronunciation may be.

Once, in a critical moment, an unusual concomitant—a man's skin color—served as a life-saving context for me.

I took part in an important international conference as a simultaneous interpreter. Like most simultaneous interpreters, I usually work at such conferences with my eyes closed so that I exclude all visual impressions and can concentrate entirely on the spoken text. One of the delegates came up with an economic policy proposal that I felt was racially discriminatory. Someone replied in clear, fine French, but I didn't catch the decisive word in his short comment; I didn't understand if he considered the proposal "acceptable" or "inacceptable." I opened my eyes, frightened, and was rescued: the speaker's pitch-black African face removed all doubt.

I will discuss vocabulary again because it is the most concrete and tangible part of knowledge.

I heard from a proud father recently that his daughter was studying German and that she was "around halfway at the moment." "What do you mean by halfway?" I asked. "Well, now she knows around 1500 words and when she learns 1500 more, she will speak German perfectly."

I only heard a more naïve remark—also in connection with German—from a fellow average language learner. Let it serve as his excuse that he must have been only 7–8 years old. He was talking to his mother on the tram:

"Mom, I imagine we'll have German class tomorrow."

Mom, obviously absorbed in her own problems, acknowledged the big event only with an absent-minded nod. The young lad, however, seemed to be very excited about it because he started to speak again after a couple of minutes:

"And tell me, mom, when the class ends, will I then speak German?"

No, little boy, unfortunately you won't. Not even after weeks, months, or perhaps years. And not even when you have the 3000 words allegedly sufficient for knowledge at your fingertips.[78]

Vocabulary, according to Gyula Laziczius,[79] is a shore-less sea unceasingly swollen inside by the possibility of word reformulation and creation, and expanded outside by contacts with other languages.

Fortunately, even before you start flirting with a new language, you may know some of its vocabulary. I counted 14 Italian words in one column of a music review last week. Our soccer fans practically quarrel in English over the details of last Sunday's match. Sputnik and its sister satellites entered public knowledge once and for all in Russian. But even from such an outsider language as Japanese, you already know what you call clothes (*kimono*), hurricane (*typhoon*), artist (*geisha*), good-bye (*sayonara*); you know "(may you live) 10,000 years" from *banzai*, "belly" and "cutting" from *hara-kiri*, and even "butterfly" from *Cio-Cio-Fujin* [*Madame Butterfly*].

Foreign languages have given us many geographical and scientific terms, among others. The only problem is that when we adopt such words, we treat them by our own language's rules. Unfortunately, the words often undergo such changes that it would take a clever philologist to recognize their original meaning sometimes.

Not long ago someone was bet that nearly all the words in a piece of English medical writing had their origin in the international Latin-Greek vocabulary. He read an excerpt in front of physicians who didn't speak English: none of them

---

78. It has been shown that we need a vocabulary of about 3000 words to understand at least 95% of an unsimplified text before we can efficiently learn from context the other 5% (Liu Na and I. S. P. Nation [1985]. Factors affecting guessing vocabulary in context. *RELC Journal* 16 [1]: 33–42). Other studies, such as those by D. Hirsh and P. Nation (1992) and B. Laufer (1989), confirm that a vocabulary of 2000 to 3000 words provides the basis for practical language use.

79. Hungarian linguist of the 20th century.

understood anything of it. And I'm not surprised. It is indeed hard to recognize *esophagus* from "isuffegs," *psyche* from "sikee," and *fetus* from "feets." The Russian words *natyurmort* (nature morte, still life) or *shedevr* (chef-d'œuvre, masterpiece) won't provide aid to those speaking French, either.

Understanding high-level, written texts is easier. However, as you learn the vocabulary of everyday life, words become more and more context-specific. There is nothing you can do about it: you have to learn them. You can't weave a fabric without thread.

14

How to Learn Words

≈

THE BASIS of classic vocabulary learning is making a glossary. You record the words to be learned from a lesson in one column of your notebook and write the equivalent terms in your mother tongue in the other. Now you cover one column with your palm, then the other; the eyes look at the words, the mouth murmurs them, and the mind is said to memorize them. This method is almost as old as language learning itself. Its disadvantage is that it carries isolated words to the brain, removed from their contexts. And the meaning to which you attach each word to be learned is your mother-tongue's meaning of the term. That is the only nail you hang your new possession on—or to put it more scientifically, that is what you associate it with. Not the healthiest start.

Among other reasons, it is not a good start because only one meaning of the word is recorded. For example, if I state in my glossary that the word *marble* means limestone, I have only recorded a half-truth because it is used at least as many times to mean crystallized rock. Large dictionaries explain words in several contexts. If you only record one meaning of a word, you deprive it of its *Hintergrund*, background.

This method, however, has a great advantage. It is *you* who have compiled the glossary—you have personal experiences associated with it. The terms on the pages crop up in your memory embedded in the context of *your self*. They recall the setting where you encountered them, the time, and sometimes even the mood in which they were jotted down.

I recommend untidy glossaries with all my heart to everyone. Neatly inscribed lines with uniform pearly letters are like desert landscapes. They mix together and make you sleepy; memory has nothing to cling to. We gain firm and steady footholds if we write with different instruments (pen, pencil, or colored pencils) in various styles (slanting, upright, small letters, capital letters, etc.).

The advantage of a glossary, thus, is its personal nature.

The other method—which is, interestingly, quite widespread—is the dictionary method. It was applied by the Orientalist Ármin Vámbéry and the poet Attila József. They both waded through complete dictionaries and that was how they got hold of the necessary vocabulary to learn languages.

A modern dictionary provides words in context. That may be why the dictionary method proves fairly successful in practice, even though it runs counter to most modern language-learning pedagogies. I have long been searching for the reason why this seemingly absurd method is so efficient.

I asked a secondary school acquaintance who learned enough German to succeed as a tourist in Germany. He replied that it was the initial letters of words that formed his associative basis; from those, he could memorize words. He learned each word's various meanings, assembled them into phrases, and the relationships revealed the inner logic of the language to him.

You can unite the logic of a dictionary and the personal feature of a glossary if you record the word to be learned in context in your notebook. You can also add words with similar meanings (synonyms) or opposite meanings (antonyms). You shouldn't force the addition; only add the words that you know are natural "associates" of the word in question.

Monkeys and apes are called higher primates because, among other things, they can use their forelegs as hands. Humans became giants because, among other things, they learned how to work with their hands. Therefore, it is no wonder that the richest group of words in all languages comes from the word *hand*. According to a German scholar, each and every variant of human activity can be expressed with the derivations of this single word. I haven't checked to see if this is so, but in French at least, a little bunch can be collected from it (Fr: *main*).

abolition	*manumission*
affected	*maniéré*
begging	*manche*
crank	*manivelle*
cuff	*manchette*
demonstration	*manifestation*
demonstrator	*manifestant*
to emancipate	*émanciper*
handcuffs	*menottes*
handle	*manche*
to handle	*manier*
handling	*manutention*
horse training	*manège*
to maintain	*maintenir*
mandate	*mandat*
manifesto	*manifeste*
manipulation	*manipulation*
manual	*manuel*
manual labor/er	*main-d'œuvre*
manufacture	*manufacture*
manuscript	*manuscrit*
muff	*manchon*
now	*maintenant*
one-armed man	*manchot*
operator	*manipulant*

to rework	*remanier*
sleeve	*manche*
slovenly	*démanché*
to transfer	*mandater*
way, manner	*manière*
etc.	

Probably all of my fellow language learners have noticed that some words stick easier in the mind than others. This depends on subjective and objective factors. The subjective factor can be simply expressed like this: you memorize the word that you have a personal connection to. An expression, a number, a name, or an event will become more fixed in your mind the more meaningful it is to you.

Here I return to my opinion again that the knowledge you obtain at the expense of some brainwork will be more yours than what you receive ready-made. If you figure it out from the context, this small incident will be a positive experience.

In addition, consider Pavlov's principle, albeit in primitive form: if two areas of the brain react at the same time, the effect is always more lasting. In language learning, the intellectual sphere can react with the emotional one. If the target language can stimulate both, the learning effect is enhanced.

Objective factors in language learning are independent of your approach and are in the word itself. You can learn most easily nouns that refer to a specific object (house, window, book, pencil). Then come adjectives denoting perceptible properties (color, form, size). Then follow abstract nouns, and then verbs that express an easily imaginable, specific action (run, give, bring). In my experience, verbs expressing a symbolic action are the hardest to learn (complete, ensure, refer).

Verbs are so far down this list because they constitute the word-class with the most changeable form. They crop up in the present tense, the past, the singular, the plural, the active form, the passive form, the conditional, and the imperative. (And we haven't even touched upon aspect [e.g., the progressive and perfect aspects in English], the imperfective and perfective forms in Russian [a great pitfall of the language], mood, etc.)

Apart from a word's meaning, its form also plays a role in how easily it can be memorized. You get in trouble with long words because with more letters, the more likely you are to have some similar letter combination lurking in the back of your mind. At such times, it is cross-association that makes you uncertain: you can easily mix them up. By the way, it holds for both words and languages that you mostly confuse what is lurking. What you are certain of is waiting to be revived neatly arranged in the multi-drawer wardrobe of your memory.

According to several educators, the danger of cross-association of similar words should be avoided by keeping them away from pupils' minds. However, I prefer lining them up and interrogating them. There are three verbs in Japanese, *okiru*, *okoru*, and *okuru*, which altogether have 10 meanings: get up, wake up, happen, rise, get angry, occur, see off, give as a present, send, and escort. I tried to avoid confusing them for a month by ignoring their similarity. I didn't succeed, and the only way I eventually managed to put them in order was by summoning them all for questioning at the same time.

Words don't only differ from each other in how easily they can be memorized; they also differ in importance. You will need "Please…" 10 times more often than "big," "big" 100 times more often than "appearance," and "appearance" 1000 times more often than "orangutan." Unfortunately, you will most often need "Excuse me?" Obviously, that will be the first thing you will say when addressed by a foreigner; logically, that is what every course book should begin with. Yet, I haven't seen even one that says how to express this vitally important question for the beginning student.

Our course books used to suffer from "substantivitis," an excess of nouns. It is understandable because nouns are the easiest vocabulary element to acquire. In the Ollendorff course books of the early 20th century, no sentence was let off without a triple possessive construction (the thoroughbred riding horse of the poacher of the neighbor's land).

Let me include a short list of words you will need if you want to make contact with someone who doesn't speak your mother tongue:

Contact-making words	Hello. Excuse me? Thank you. Please. I'm sorry. Good morning, good afternoon, good evening. Good-bye.
Ready-made formulas	I'm from the U.S. Where is…? Do you speak…? Please say it again. Slower please. I don't speak…
Pronouns	I. You. Whose? Mine, yours… Who? What? This, that.
Adverbs of place, time, etc.	Here. There. Where? To the right. To the left. Straight on. Already. Yet. Still. Now. When? How many? How much? Many, much, few, little, more.
Auxiliary words	Have to, must. May. Can. I'd like… Why? Because…
Inflected forms of "to be" and "to have"	[Language dependent]
Numbers	From one till ten, till a hundred. Days of the week, names of the months. Today, tomorrow, etc.

Important verbs	Leave. Arrive. Come, go. Start, finish. Eat, drink, look for, find, buy, get on, get off, have, know.
Nouns	It is a difficult question as their priority depends on the situation. For a tourist: room, bed, bathroom. In a restaurant: soup, bread, meat, water, beer, pasta. If you have some money for shopping, you don't have to do anything but point. You will be understood.
Adjectives in the positive and comparative degree	Big, small. Cheap, expensive. Hot, cold. Good, bad.

This list, of course, can be extended and reduced at will. You can also play with it by checking how many forms you can instantly express in their foreign equivalents.

Unfortunately, there are a host of expressions that play a greater role in making you fluent than verbs, nouns, adjectives, and all other "responsible" word-classes. I call them filler words because their common property is that they don't change the essence of a sentence, they only supplement it.

Such filler words are *quite, obviously, rather, of course, well, in fact, though, mostly, certainly, instead, a lot, still, anyway,* etc. It is not easy to memorize them because there are no objective concepts attached to them, yet I recommend learning them with all my heart.

Since we are discussing filler words, let's not forget filling clauses, either. These are usually sentence-launching expressions, not even bricks of the building of language, but in fact ready-made slabs of it. They can be carried to the spot in prefabricated forms and plastered in immediately. Their great advantage is that they provide transitions between banal discourse and important discourse. In addition, they allow you time to recall expressions that have sunk deep into your memory. You can then strike the tuning fork, which I have mentioned several times.

I have also mentioned that adults—as opposed to children—don't learn texts verbatim easily or willingly. Even if your mind has aversions to cramming fairly long coherent pieces, don't be shy of compiling and learning launching expressions. I have a notebook of them for each of my languages; I keep them updated with constant additions. My source is not only my readings, but also what I learn from my partners:

> The fact is that...
> I would like to specifically point out...
> Let's consider especially...
> That reminds me,...
> On the other hand, however,...
> Of course I know that...
> It is also true that...
> Not mentioning the fact that...
> We should not forget that...

As a group unto themselves, these launching expressions are unpleasantly sticky and gluey. But used in front of a sentence, they are lubricants. Their role is to make the delivery of the more important parts of a message smoother and more acceptable.

And anyway, my dear reader, all I want to say is that we shouldn't forget that we are dealing with a foreign language, and in a foreign (unknown) language environment, we are often glad to be alive at all.

15

Age and Language Learning

≈

I MUST begin this chapter by challenging two common assumptions. The first is that children are exceptional language learners. It is not true.

According to István Terts,[80] an average language course consists of 600 lessons. And so it may be—for the average adolescent or adult. It is commonly assumed that a child can learn a language faster, at least his first, because he or she has the advantage of not having to replace an established code system with another. However, if you exclude infancy and calculate eight waking hours a day, the child may need five years to satisfy the linguistic requirement of the first grade—almost 20 times as much as the average number of lessons quoted above. This is because a school's way of assessing readiness is typically a poor measure of the personal knowledge the child has acquired in his natural environment.

The word *personal* should be emphasized because a six-year-old doesn't really know concepts and categories. A school's way of assessing readiness can be to show a young candidate images of a cat and a dog or an apple and a pear. The child will usually recognize them, but if he can't tell that he has seen an *animal* in the first case and a *fruit* in the second, he is usually encouraged to remain in kindergarten

---

80. Hungarian linguist (b. 1948).

for one more year.

Of course, we should consider the connection between age and language learning with more tolerance. After all, a component of language knowledge, pronunciation, can hardly be acquired after the age of 10 or 11.

Henry Kissinger, one of the most intelligent people of our age, is a prime example. He arrived in the New World at the age of 15. Fifty years later, when he was giving a lecture at Stanford University, a professor correctly identified him as being from the Franconian part of Germany.

After learning 16 languages and after more than half a century of living in Budapest, sharp-eared people can still discover in my speech the vowels typical of natives of Baranya.[81]

The most favorable time to enrich vocabulary and improve conceptual ability is adolescence. However, I would prefer to postpone learning grammar rather than try to learn it the way it is prescribed in present-day curricula.

Grammar is the most abstract field in the realm of the intellect. As I usually put it, "I will sooner see a UFO than a dative case or a subject complement." When learning spelling, it is helpful to acquire the letter-sound relationships, but there is no need to clarify the specific types of inflectional and derivational suffixes. A Hungarian won't say *szobában* even if the rule of vowel assimilation has never been explained to him or her.[82] The mother tongue is such a natural medium for thought as a field is for a wild flower.

When learning a foreign language, however, grammar can be a catalyst. If a student wishes to get his bearings in our Hungarian language, it will be a pleasant surprise for

---

81. A county in southern Hungary. Its seat, Pécs, where Dr. Lomb was born, is approximately 120 miles south of Budapest.

82. In Hungarian, most suffixes have two or three variants (e.g., *-ban* and *-ben* for "in") and their use depends on whether a word contains front or back vowels. *Szoba* (room) contains back vowels so the *-ban* version should be used with it.

him that all attributive adjectives can be transformed into nouns with the suffix *-ság/-ség*, e.g.,

szép	→	*szép**ség*** (niceness)
csúnya	→	*csúnya**ság*** (ugliness)
gazdag	→	*gazdag**ság*** (richness)
szegény	→	*szegény**ség*** (poorness)

The student of German can envy the student of Hungarian because there are four different suffixes for this transformation in German: *Schön**heit**, Hässlich**keit**, Reich**tum**, Ar**mut**.*

But I must voice my opinion again that a rule you have realized for yourself will take a much deeper root in you than a rule served ready-made by a course book or teacher. The same applies, of course, to vocabulary. The expression deciphered from the context doesn't only mean a new piece of knowledge, but also a sense of achievement, which is the key to success in all learning—and maybe to life.

Intellectual opportunities of old age

The second false assumption about age and language learning is that "you can but forget in old age, not learn anymore." It would be sad if that were the case. From one who has thought deeply about the question, and experienced a fleeting youth and overworked adulthood, it is the years of retirement that provide the opportunity to do what you are actually interested in at a pace of your own liking.

I have a problem even with the terminology of old age. It is politely called *troisième âge* in French and "golden years" in English. In Hungarian, I prefer teenagers' parlance: *"Na, öregem, mit szólsz a tegnapi Fradi-meccshez?"*[83]

---

83. "Well, dude, what do you think of Fradi's [a popular soccer team] match yesterday?" ("Dude" is used for *öregem* [lit., my old one] here.)

Without a doubt, the duration of old age is gradually becoming longer.

In 1526, after the disaster at Mohács,[84] the Council of Elders was assembled to resolve the fate of the country in ruins. Its oldest member was 40.

Hippocrates was called "venerable ancestor" by his young students when he reached the age of 45. By the way, he may have outlived them all: according to the *Encyclopædia Britannica*, he died at the age of 110, in the third century B.C.

Thanks to the development of medicine, the years of the alleged intellectual vacuum may lengthen into decades in the approaching new century. How do we view the intellectual opportunities of old age?

I think with a certain openness. As we age, details will undoubtedly become blurred but our perspective will become broader. Outlines of categories solidify and the individual details within them reduce in sharpness.

As age advances, we forget the details behind which there are no logical connections. First of all, names. There are several jokes about our failure to remember names. The fact that anxiety plays a role in such lapses is shown by the banal irony that we often remember a name long after we have been thinking hard to recall it.

How can we protect ourselves against this undeniable disadvantage of advanced age? First of all, by associating the name (word) with something. Even the most primitive ways can work. The fact that the neighbor's granddaughter is called *Lilla* can be associated with her birth in May, when lilacs appear.

I cannot recommend highly enough to keep such launching expressions in stock. Their function is like that of sprinting in the pole vault: momentum to clear the bar. He

---

84. A decisive defeat by the Ottomans, an event of symbolic importance in the history of Hungary.

who stops at the pit and throws himself up into the air with a "whoop!" will certainly knock the bar down.

Perspective on the soul and essence of language is a privilege of old age.

An excellent means to avoid failure in language learning is to practice monologues. This parlor game may become an established method to enrich and solidify your vocabulary: who can list more words with a similar meaning (synonyms)? The latest competition I participated in was like that: who has the largest stock of synonyms for the English word *drunk*? I reached the final with the words *fuddled*, *tipsy*, *inebriated*, and *high*, and I won hands down with the terms *blotto*, *pifflicated*, and *intoxicated*. The only reason I didn't come away with a gold medal was that I was competing all by myself; it took place on a night coach to Rome when I couldn't fall asleep due to the clatter…

16

Dictionaries: Crutches or
Helpful Tools?

≈

ANATOLE FRANCE called dictionaries "a universe arranged in alphabetical order." I admit I cannot take one into my hands—even after all these years—without a fluttering heart.

Our trade is a fortunate one. One movement of the hand in a dictionary is enough to get a quick solution to your problem. One second—and you will know what you want. Just consider how many experiments, how much debate and brainwork it takes to answer a question in several other fields from theosophy to nuclear physics!

A dictionary is a long-term means to quench your thirst for knowledge. It deserves a couple of thoughts for the thousands of words accumulated in it.

The first thing I'd like to tell my fellow language students is to use dictionaries. The second is not to abuse them.

To spring open the lock of a language, a dictionary is an excellent key. The learner should buy one, leaf through it, and use it till it is dog-eared. The condition called "well-thumbed" in English means that the owner of a book has thoroughly made use of the information it provides.

Dictionary use is also the best way to acquire a non-Romanized alphabet. Even my acquaintances with an average linguistic interest (I deliberately didn't write linguistic gift, as I don't believe in it) put down the Russian dictionary after half a day, having figured out the "secrets" of the Cyrillic alphabet based on international words. What can the word MOTOP [motor] mean? Or MOCKBA [Moscow]? And if they were then driven by curiosity as far as POTOP [rotor] or CAMOBAP [samovar], the joy of the verification of their ideas certainly fixed the knowledge in them for all their lifetime.

Knowing how to use a dictionary is the most urgent task of a learner in regards to time, too. I would immediately put one into the hands of those dealing with "hieroglyphic" languages like Chinese or Japanese.

Then I would take it away from them. And from other language students as well.

Because in the initial—almost pre-linguistic—phase, a dictionary inspires thinking but later on, it positively makes you stop. Unfortunately, one tends to use it instead of thinking. Its being easy to use lures you to laziness: I've bought it, it's at hand, I'll look it up. How much simpler it is than racking your brains for a word!

But there is no learning without some mild brainwork. At the very beginning of dealing with a language, a dictionary can be inspiring; later on, it motivates you to follow the way of least resistance.

What should you do then, if an expression doesn't come into your mind when reading a book, doing homework, composing, translating, etc.? Should you not use a dictionary? Well, you should, but wisely.

The word you are looking for usually rings in your ears in some way. Oh, what is "hair" called in French? You reach for the English-French dictionary and look it up. Annoyed, you strike your forehead—of course it's *cheveux*!—and you forget it again immediately.

However, if you start from the vague scraps recalled from the mist of your memory (*che... chev...*) and you take the trouble to ascertain it from a reverse (French-English) dictionary, the reward of congratulating yourself will help the word become fixed in your mind. Twice as much time consumed, 10 times better efficiency.

Even at an elementary level of language knowledge, you can use monolingual or learner's dictionaries. The Russian Usakov, the French Larousse, the English Oxford, and the German Duden are examples. The principle of more energy invested equals better efficiency especially applies here.

Let's suppose you are racking your brain for the Russian equivalent of "exact." It is dawning on you that there is a better term for it than *аккуратный* (*akkuratnyy*), which arises spontaneously in your memory. Instead of the too-easy way of looking it up in a Hungarian-Russian dictionary, it is much more effective to look up *аккуратный* in a Russian dictionary. Finding *точный* (*tochnyy*) in it will mean it will be fixed in your memory 10 times more effectively.

Today's dictionaries don't reflect Anatole France's universe in mere headwords. With their phrases and sample sentences, entries are positively readable today. The meanings of words are illuminated by their contexts. In fact, there is no other way to show them.

A good dictionary is a rich treasury of "-isms" (Russianisms, Germanisms, etc.). By providing words not in isolation but in various contexts, it creates new opportunities to memorize them. Whenever the same word crops up in a new phrase, it will be fixed in your mind in yet another way. Thus the *sentence* provided by the dictionary is a reliable unit worthy of learning. On the other hand, a *word* is not a reliable unit of learning because its meaning may depend on its context. A long and coherent text is not a reliable unit of learning either, because it is simply too much for the average person to absorb.

17

Textbooks

≈

WE HAVE made a huge advance in this field. Hungarians can now learn any language from course books based on modern pedagogical principles. However, I believe that Hungarians should learn from a book prepared by a Hungarian. This is not owing to chauvinism but because speakers of different languages face different challenges when learning a foreign language. Jespersen, the eminent Danish philologist, knew this: he classified the errors committed in English by nationality.

Let me cite an example to support my view. After the liberation,[85] the first Russian course book used in Hungary was Potapova's. Glancing through it, I wondered why the book dealt extensively with certain language points quite natural for us Hungarians while it barely touched upon certain others. For instance, it included several sentences to help us learn the rule that the word "where" (*где*) should be expressed in Russian differently than "to where" (*куда*).[86] I couldn't understand why they had to go on about this fact,

---

85. In 1945, when the Soviets liberated Hungary from the Germans and at the same time occupied it.
86. This difference is not consistently expressed in English either, cf. "Where are you?" (place) and "Where are you going?" (direction; theoretically "where to").

self-evident to us, until I realized that the book had been originally written for the French. Because there are no separate words in French for "where" and "where to" (both translate as *où*), the book stressed a linguistic point that is natural for us, one which we can't even imagine in another way.

Even though it is sometimes fashionable at higher levels, it is wrong when elementary school textbooks from a foreign country are used as language course books. It is true that from the point of view of language knowledge an adult student is a child, but he or she is a child in a different way. First, a six-year-old child studies his elementary school textbook primarily to gain literacy. Second, these textbooks can be so culturally bound or dated as to be useless. I once came across one in a village in Hajdú county that began *"A kanász a tülökkel riog."* (The swineherd is hooting with a horn.)

Now what would a Polish, Russian, or French student of Hungarian do with that?

18

How We Converse in a Foreign Language

≈

INITIALLY, we converse in a foreign language by translating words from our mother tongue to the foreign language. As we get more proficient, we adapt knowledge directly to the appropriate forms and structures of the foreign language.

Thus we make connections *between* languages or *within* a language, or both.

This instinct helps us acquire the language *and* can make it more difficult.

By the time an adolescent or adult begins to study his first foreign language, the complexities of language have already begun to live within him. Although he may not be completely conscious of it, he will have some idea of singular and plural forms; the present, past, and future tenses; the difference between action and occurrence; and the hundred different ways thought can be transformed into expression. The learner will automatically extrapolate this knowledge when studying a new language.

For example, the learner will understand that the forms of the verb "to read" will have parallel forms in most other languages.

to read	reading	reader	read
olvasni	olvasás	olvasó	olvasott
lesen	das Lesen	der Leser	gelesen
читать	чтение	читатель	прочитанный
lire	la lecture	le lecteur	lu
....	....	....	....
....	....	....	....

etc.

These two activities—recognizing forms between languages and morphing them within a language—enable you to get your bearings in the labyrinth of a foreign language.

Now, these two functions would solve all our problems if languages were regular, fixed systems that followed uniform laws. Unfortunately, they are not, because what is used by many will inevitably change.

Language is a tool used for millions of purposes. Its change is natural: it stretches and it wears away, it widens and it shrinks. It loses its regular shape. And it loses its shape where it is touched by the most people: at everyday words. And everyday words are what all language learners must deal with.

What kinds of everyday words have changed? Our language teachers have compiled a list of the 40 most frequently used English verbs (do, take, go, come, eat, drink, etc.). Almost all of them are irregular.

We must recognize that colloquialisms, which are an essential part of any language, are made up of everyday words. Colloquialisms are more difficult to learn and use than most academic and technical expressions. It is easier to understand a technical text than to correctly ask for a glass of water, or tell a good joke.

Academic and technical expressions tend to be international and easy to recognize, at least in writing. By extrapolating and interpolating, we can follow meaning closely. It is relatively easy to translate a sentence about the dissolution of the protein component of protoplasm. Not only are the expressions international, but the construction of the sentence will follow a regular pattern. But woe to he who asks "what is the time" by translating the Hungarian expression.[87]

It is expressed in German as: How late is it? (*Wie spät ist es?*); in French: Which hour is it (*Quelle heure est-il?*); in Russian: Which hour? (*Который час?—Kotoryy chas?*); in English: What is the time?; in Swedish: How much is the clock? (*Hur mycket är klockan?*); in Hebrew: What is the hour? (*Mah ha shaah?*)

Language learners proceed on a bumpier road than anyone else who acquires a skill. Their way is complicated by automatic extra- and interpolation, which in linguistics is called transfer, interference, or cross-association.

Those who study engineering or medicine don't have to start their studies by suppressing already existing knowledge. They don't have ingrained, "faulty" ideas.

Just imagine how different those subjects would be if you had to set aside all your previous concepts about numbers and live with a new numeric system. How much time and energy would it take you to stop thinking that two plus two equals four?

It is in vocabulary acquisition where the mother tongue influence disturbs us the least. Even a beginner will soon understand and learn that table is not table in Spanish but *mesa* and book is not book but *libro*. But it won't be so easy to avoid answering the question "What is on the table?" as "**Allí es un libro sobre la mesa*" instead of *"Hay un libro sobre la mesa"* (There is a book on the table).

Mother-tongue interference is a well-known phenomenon. However, our language educators speak much less about the fact that many false extrapolations don't originate from one's mother tongue but from the first foreign language acquired. This occurs because when we first study a foreign language, we consciously remember its rules. When we learn a second foreign language, these rules may interfere.

---

87. The Hungarian equivalents are *"Hány óra (van)?"*—lit., "How many hours (are there)?"; or *"Mennyi az idő?"*—lit., "How much is the time?"

For example, we Hungarians who have learned English have imprinted in our minds that the consonants *p*, *t*, and *c* must be pronounced with aspiration. However, we have succeeded so well that when we switch to French, we have to consciously unlearn the rule because aspirated consonants will distort the comprehensibility of French words just like those in Hungarian.

Even if extrapolation has a certain negative impact on the acquirability of a new language, it may be a valuable means for fixing knowledge in our minds, because unfixed knowledge will fly away.

In Hungarian, the huge difference between "studying" and "learning" lies in the subtle difference of *tanulni* and *megtanulni*. There is nothing to know about this difference except that it must be fixed in one's mind.

If unfixed knowledge did not fly away, then the number of those who *study* a language would be identical to those who *learn* a language. Unfortunately, that is not the case.

You read a word or a rule but your mind only glides over it: it hasn't become your own, it hasn't become a tool that you can use as you please whenever you need it. You are lucky if you can recognize it the next time you see it.

One of the tried and true methods of fixing knowledge is contrasting. An adult mind will do it even if the most modern pedagogy turns its nose up at it.

For example, among European languages, you should remember that:

- German makes adjectives agree in gender and number with the modified words, unlike Hungarian or English.
- Polish doesn't use personal pronouns (as opposed to Russian) because the endings of verb forms will unambiguously indicate the agent.
- Spanish, in contrast with Italian and French, couples verbs expressing movement with the auxiliary verb *haber* rather than *ser*.

- English, unlike Hungarian, expresses the action going on in the present with the present perfect tense if it began in the past.[88]
- Russian, in contrast with Hungarian, uses the partitive (genitive) case after nouns expressing quantity, e.g., кусок хлеба (a piece of bread).

From a pedagogical perspective, the most valuable mistake is the one you make yourself. If I discover an error I've made or if I am taken to task for a mistake, the emotional sphere tapped will conjure wonder, annoyance, or offense. They are all excellent means of fixation.

Let's not be angry then with mistakes. Many a valuable thing were born out of them—among other things, the French, Italian, and Spanish languages. All three developed from the vulgar (common) use of Latin.

Of course, we shouldn't create new languages. But we can acquire the existing ones better by comparing the properties of the starting (mother) language and the new language.

If you place the correct and incorrect adaptations next to each other, you can avoid mistakes becoming ingrained. This is very important. The tuning fork, already mentioned several times, must ring clearly because that is what you tune the word or sentence with. This is why it is not a good idea to keep reading your uncorrected translations or compositions, and especially to learn them by heart. Only perfectly correct texts are suitable for this purpose. If you hear the wrong form several times, it will steal into your ears and make itself accepted as concert pitch.

---

88. Similarly, a speaker of English will have to remember that a sentence like "He has been writing a letter for two hours" is expressed in the present tense in several languages.

19

How We Should Converse
in a Foreign Language

≈

WE ARE sometimes told, in connection with learning a foreign language, that we should *think* in the language. I'm not comfortable with that piece of advice.

How can you state what language you are thinking in? How and when can you penetrate into the exceedingly complex mechanism of brain activity?

These things can be done only under extreme, usually tragic circumstances: when the memory of a patient breaks down—sometimes completely, sometimes partly—due to an injury to a particular part of the brain.

Our brain pathologists know of cases where the mother tongue dropped out due to an injury but foreign languages didn't. In other cases, the patient forgot only the verbs of his or her mother tongue but not the nouns. Scientific research will certainly clarify further our knowledge of the process of thinking and speaking.

We have compared speech in a foreign language to so many things—let's compare it now to photography. Let's suppose we see a beautiful rose and we want to take a photo of it. Nobody will press the lens against the individual petals and shoot them, one after another. Instead, you withdraw to a certain distance. You should go no further than what is necessary to see the whole of the rose when you glance into the viewfinder.

The language learner who wants to translate words one by one makes the same mistake as a bad photographer. The object to be photographed, to continue the metaphor, should be the complete foreign-language form—a full sentence or phrase—not a part.

As we have stated, the most tangible and quotable part of a language is vocabulary; let me refer to it again.

The terror of "I don't remember it" always hovers over you whenever you are speaking a foreign language. You won't remember a term, however, as long as you keep galloping frightened around the mother-tongue term. ("Oh my God, what is it called…?")

With practice and discipline, you can reach a stage where you banish the mother-tongue expression from your mind and you flash upon an accompanying word in the foreign language that you usually hear in conjunction with the fugitive term.

During my short career as a language instructor, I experimentally asked some pupils over a couple of lessons how the adjective "five-year" was expressed in Russian. When I asked the question in Hungarian, they hesitated; but when I helped them with the Russian word план (plan), they immediately replied with the correct answer: пятилетний (five-year). They had learned the words together; one helped recall the other.[89]

If I have recommended learning words in bunches, it is for two purposes. First, a word's relationship to others defines its meaning better. Second, it will be imprinted in your memory in context, which will help you retrieve it when you need it.

Whoever glances into the depths of the shoreless sea of

---

89. Five-year plans were national economic development plans in the satellite states of the Soviet Union.

vocabulary will be surprised at how many embracing word pairs there are in the world. Learning them is a task of the first rank, something that I wholeheartedly recommend to all learners. For example:

> An obstacle is overcome
> A duty is fulfilled
> A news story is reported
> A role is played
> A standard of living is raised
> A demand is satisfied
> A message is delivered
> A condition is created
> A wall is built (or knocked down)
> etc.

The learner who learns word pairs like these can count on the fact that when he or she is supposed to talk about a particular topic, the words will appear in the viewfinder of his or her camera. Intelligible sentences can then be produced.

What happens if both members of the pair cannot be recalled? One should use the old student escape clause: "I know it but it just slipped my mind..." and then say something similar. Yes, it is still better to say something similar and imperfect than to fall silent. Speaking a foreign language always means a compromise, Kosztolányi said.

Apart from synonyms, it is antonyms that help you most. If neither *daring, heroic, brave,* or *courageous* come to mind, *not cowardly* will still prove better than falling silent. You can also say *not flexible* instead of *rigid* or *stiff,* and *lacking dynamism* instead of *mild* or *listless.*

If you are in especially bad shape and this method won't help, you have a last resort: circumlocution. "How poetic it sounded," I once praised one of my fellow interpreters, "when you spoke about the humble little flower that is revealed by its scent from far away." "I had to say that because I forgot the word for 'violet' in Italian," she replied.

Synonyms, antonyms, and circumlocution are kind helpers when starting to speak a foreign language. They have, however, enemies and pitfalls as well: false friends. That is the name for words that appear identical or similar in meaning but are not.

Because they often entail common words, false friends are worthy of our attention. Here are two anecdotes about them.

Señor Gonzalez wished to spend a weekend in London. He brought with him the addresses of many boarding houses, yet he had to spend the night in a London park. Why? The reason is that although there were signs saying "Vacancy" on the doors of most of the boarding houses, he confused the word with the Spanish word *vacación*, which means "vacation," "shutdown," or "cease of activity." And so he only knocked on the doors where he didn't see such a notice. He was unfortunately rejected at those places.

It was in Sevilla where Signore Rossi fared badly. Trusting in the similarities between Spanish and Italian, he asked for butter for breakfast by saying "burro." After some delay, his hotel produced a beautifully harnessed donkey! (what "burro" means in Spanish). [I note in passing that a Hungarian wishing to ride a donkey from Capri to Anacapri can safely order a *somaro* because that is indeed the correct term.[90]]

False friends have caused even greater trouble. Once a Frenchman submitted a *demande* (request) at a meeting. However, a "demand" means more than a mere request in

---

90. Capri and Anacapri are townships on the Italian island of Capri. The Hungarian word for donkey is *szamár*.

English; it is an *emphatic* request. The British representative found this immodesty offensive and immediately vetoed it.

One would assume that there are no false friends at least in the world of mathematics, that numbers do speak an international language. Unfortunately, that is not the case. "Billion" is 1,000,000 × 1,000,000, a million times a million, expressed as 10^{12} in most European countries. In the States, however, it is only 1,000 × 1,000,000, a thousand times a million, expressed as 10^9. This figure is called *milliard* in most parts of Europe.

Titles, ranks, and school types are indicated differently in different countries. A Hungarian *akadémikus* (academician, member of the Academy of Sciences) is not the same as a German *Akademiker* because the latter is only someone who has graduated from a university or college. A university or college is called *Hochschule* in German but "high school" refers to a secondary school in America—roughly like *gimnázium* in Hungarian. *Gymnasium,* on the other hand, means a sport facility in English and comes from the Greek word *gymnos* (naked).

When I learned that the father of my friend in Madrid had a car accident, I inquired about his health by phone. *"Esperamos su muerte,"* I was told. I hung up in shock. It was only later when I realized that the verb *esperar* means "to wait" or "to expect," not just "to hope" like the French *espérer.*[91] I also learned that the one said to be *prematuramente jubilado* did not jubilate (rejoice) too soon but retired early. On the other hand, it was a pleasant surprise that the Hungarian *cédula* (note, slip of paper) is also *cédula* in Spanish (document) and a scribe is a *chupatintas.*[92]

The Hungarian word *kokett* was used to mean "coquett-

---

91. In other words, Lomb mistook "We expect his death" for "We hope for his death."

92. *"Chupatintas"* sounds like *csupatintász* in Hungarian (someone with ink all over him or her; not an actual word but a formation that can be understood by all its elements).

ish" when I was young. Its French meaning is much more general: e.g., *une somme coquette*—a tidy sum.

I am angry with English because "he blames himself" doesn't mean *blamálja magát* (to make a fool of oneself, to disgrace oneself) and I am disappointed with Spanish because *compromiso* is not only a compromise but a commitment or engagement.

The following blunder occurred in a Hungarian-Polish business deal. A cosmetics factory in Warsaw believed it had invented a miraculous anti-wrinkle face cream; it offered its marketing in Hungary to a foreign trade company of ours. Correspondence took place in French; the Polish client called the agent of the cream *agent à dérider* (*ride*: wrinkle). Her Hungarian partner conscientiously looked up the words in the dictionary and established that *agent* means "a police officer" and *dérider* "detection." The trade company stated by mail that "such things are outside the profile of our company."

In the Netherlands one should be careful with the word *monster* because it means "sample," in contrast to its meaning in English. "Be careful" is, on the other hand, *Andacht* in Dutch. *Andacht* in German, however, means devotion. I would have certainly translated the Portuguese word *importância* as "importance" had I not realized from the context that it means amount.

An Italian beau will not succeed if he flatters a German girl by saying that he finds her *calda* and *morbida* (warm and soft), because *calda* connotes *kalt* (cold) and *morbida* connotes *morbidität* (morbid). A Frenchman should not praise the beautiful *denture* of his English partner either; it means natural teeth in his language but the opposite in English.

In a foreign language conversation (or composition or translation), your partner wants to get a faithful image of your message. It is a self-evident and primitive truth that this faithfulness can be least ensured by the literal transfer of your language forms to your partner's language. If we take sticking to the mother tongue to absurdity, we could state that German fighters give each other foot-treads (*Fußtritt*) and earfigs (*Ohrfeige*): no one would suspect that we meant to say "kicks" and "slaps."

Many commonplaces have been mentioned in connection with translation. The most commonplace of commonplaces goes like this: "the translation that is good sticks to the original in the most faithful way possible but at the same time gives the exact impression of having been written in the target language." Let me rephrase this as "the transfer (speech, translation, interpreting) that is good evokes the same associations that the original intended to evoke."

Note that those who want this level of transfer, however, will sometimes go too far. That is what happened to me at a banquet that a minister of ours arranged in honor of his Japanese colleague. I sat at the table as an interpreter.

Fish was served as an appetizer. The guest, for the purpose of *captatio benevolentiae* (capturing the benevolence), started the conversation this way: "My solidarity with the working class was decided for life by having crab for dinner every evening until I was 18."

If I were a humorist, I would write that my fork froze in my mouth. But in fact I turned pale: if I translated the sentence word for word, I would make a blunder. What the proletariat eats every day in Japan is served at gourmet banquets in Hungary.

I hereby apologize to all lexicographers. All I could do was translate the gentleman's sentence this way: "My solidarity with the working class was decided for life by having roux soup for dinner every evening until I was 18."

20

How I Learn Languages

≈

NOW THAT I have given you some theory, I would like to relate how I actually go about learning a language. I pass on my strategies in the hope that those who are smarter than me will propose different, more effective strategies that I can add to my own.

Let's say that I wish to learn Azilian. There is no such language, of course. I have made it up to emphasize the general approach I use to learn any language.

First of all, I try to get my hands on a thick Azilian-Hungarian dictionary. Owing to my optimistic outlook I never buy small dictionaries; I go on the assumption that they are a waste of money because I would fathom them too quickly. If an Azilian-Hungarian dictionary is not available, then I try to get hold of an Azilian-English, Azilian-Russian, etc., dictionary.

In the beginning, I use this dictionary as my textbook. I learn the rules of reading from it. Every language—and consequently every dictionary—contains a lot of international expressions. The bigger the dictionary, the more such expressions there are in it.

The words for nations and cities (that is, places that do not have language-dependent names) and scientific terms that transcend specific languages reveal to me the relationships between letter-characters and phonemes in Azilian. I remember that the first thing I looked up in the Russian-English dictionary I bought in 1941 was my own name: *Екатерина.*[93]

I do not memorize words from the dictionary; I just scan and study them as though they were some crossword puzzle to be solved. By the time I glean the rules of reading from the above-cited international words, the dictionary will have revealed a lot of other things about Azilian. For example, I can see how it morphs the parts of speech: how it nominalizes verbs, how it forms adjectives from nouns, and how it forms adverbs from adjectives.

This is just a first taste of the language. I am sampling it, making friends with it.

Following this first assay, I buy a textbook and some works of Azilian literature. Regarding textbooks, I always buy one with the answers provided for the exercises, as I am an average language learner: i.e., I mostly have to teach myself.

I go through the lessons and complete all the exercises in sequence, as they come in the book. I write breezily, leaving ample room for corrections. Then I look up the answers in the key and write them beside/above my own incorrect responses. In this way I get a visual representation of "the history of my folly."[94]

I scold myself for the errors made and then promptly forgive myself. (This is very important; see the 10th Commandment on page 160.) I always leave enough space in my notebook to write five–six correct words or sentences for the ones I got wrong. This is very helpful in imprinting the correct formulas.

As all this is a bit tedious, right from the outset I start reading Azilian plays or short stories. If I get lucky, there will

---

93. This transcribes as Yekaterina, the equivalent of Catherine.
94. This is a reference to the title of a romantic Hungarian movie.

be adapted texts available. If not, I just start on any literature published before 1950. (I can have trouble understanding the style of modern novels, even in Hungarian.) I always buy books in pairs: this increases the chance that at least one will be comprehensible.

I start on the comprehensible novel immediately. To go from incomprehension to half-understanding to complete understanding is an exciting and inspiring journey of discovery worthy of the spirit of a mature person. By the time I finish the journey, I part with the book feeling that this has been a profitable and fun enterprise.

On my first reading of the book, I write words I understand into my notebook; that is, words whose meaning I have been able to figure out from the context. Naturally, I do not write them out in isolation, but in sentences. It is only after a second or third reading that I look up words I don't know. Even then, I do not look up every one. For those that I record in my notebook, I include the context from the book or from a contemporary dictionary worthy of the name.

Verbal comprehension

All this, however, does not teach one of the most important of the four aspects of language learning: verbal comprehension. What's more, I have not gotten an accurate picture of Azilian pronunciation, because the phonetic transcriptions of the textbook are always of somewhat dubious value. For this reason, at the beginning of my language study I set aside some time for scanning the Azilian airwaves. I figure out when and at what frequency I can hear Azilian speech on the radio. Somewhere, sometime, I am sure to catch it from the ether.

News bulletins generally present the most important international events of the day. Therefore, even if the news items are selected according to the probable interests of Azilians, they will likely be the same on different stations, in different languages. So I always listen to the news in some other, familiar language as well. Thus I am given a key—almost a dictionary—to what I can expect, in advance. If an unknown word crops up along the way, I write it down. After the broadcast, I look it up immediately in my big dictionary. The reason for this is that right after the broadcast, the word is still resounding in my ear with its entire context. If I misheard it (which happens many times), the context, still fresh in my memory, helps me correct the error.

If I find the word in the dictionary, a little self-congratulation is in order again, and this makes learning a pleasant pastime instead of a burdensome task.

Then, not immediately, but after a day or two, I record in my glossary the knowledge acquired off the air. I recommend this temporally staggered approach because one is forced to revisit fading memories—unfortunately, quite often not for the last time.

Once a week, I tape the broadcast. I keep the recording for a while and play it back several times. On these occasions, I always concentrate on pronunciation. Alas, I must admit that based on the announcer's native pronunciation, sometimes I have to reacquaint myself with words that I thought I already knew from books.

Of course, I try to find a teacher who speaks Azilian. If I find a professional educator, I've got it made. If there isn't a bona fide teacher available, I try to at least find an Azilian who is in Hungary on a scholarship.

Gender and language use

I confess that I prefer being taught by a woman. Perhaps this is because it is easier to chat with women. I have long been intrigued by the question of why women talk more than men.

In connection with this fact, let me theorize a bit about the problem of women's language vs. men's language.

They say that women are more loose-tongued. I read in

books on archeology that women's skeletons are characterized as much by their more delicate, more finely chiseled
jaws as by their broader hip bones. It is a fact that generally
women everywhere speak faster than men do. (According to
Mario Pei, the average American male utters 150 syllables
per minute, while the average American female utters 175.)
Countless jokes, clichés, and comedy routines have been
based on the fact that women talk more. This "verbal infla-
tion" is expressed in different ways in different languages,
based on a woman's age and social status.

For example, a little girl "prattles." By the time she gets
to school, she "chatters" or "jabbers"; when she grows up she
"babbles." A lady "chats," a female colleague "yakety-yaks"
or perhaps "blabs," a neighbor "gabbles," a bride "twitters,"
a wife "blathers," a mother-in-law "cackles." A girl-buddy is
reprimanded and told to cut the "chinfest." And so on.

Let me interject here, in connection with tongues, what
I think accounts for the cliché *Ein Mann ist ein Wort; eine
Frau ist ein Wörterbuch* (A man is a word; a woman is a dic-
tionary).

Prehistoric man's meals came from killing prehistoric
buffalo. Owing to the stronger male physique, it was natural
that men would go hunting while women stayed at home.
Not to mention the fact that pregnancy and nursing pretty
much filled a woman's life and she would not survive her
fertile years by much. This was slow to change; even at the
turn of the 20th century, the average life expectancy of a
woman was only 50 years.

Today we are aware that the brain is compartmental-
ized: there exists a particular division of labor between the
two hemispheres. The right brain governs motion while the
left brain plays the decisive role in governing speech and
verbal activity.

It is no wonder that in women the right brain has regressed—if not in volume, at least in function—because
women move less. At the same time, the left brain, respon-

sible for verbalization/vocalization, has grown in importance. Seventy-five percent of all interpreters, worldwide, are women.

The ideogrammatic part of the Japanese character set reflects the meanings of words. The "hieroglyph" for "man" is "人" because a man walks on two legs and feet and emerges from the animal kingdom with a straight torso. The symbol for "woman," by contrast, is "女"—a woman sits and doesn't walk.

As a result of the decreased need and opportunity for moving about, women's capacity for spatial orientation has regressed. In keeping with this, the radius of their sphere of interest has also gotten smaller. It has focused on their immediate environment: people. Let us think of a camera: one narrows its aperture when focusing on nearby objects rather than faraway landscapes.

As a result of this shortening of perspective, women follow personal relationships more closely, recognize their patterns more readily, and talk about them more frequently.

Women have a closer relationship to words. It is therefore logical that the number of women authors is on the rise. It is also interesting to note that their importance is increasing, especially in the field of fiction. Although emotions are well expressed by poetry, this genre requires more pithy, concise forms. With all due apologies to our excellent Hungarian women poets, women's greater affinity with words can gain a more auspicious manifestation in the more loquacious genre of prose. I am proud to cite Endre Bajomi Lázár's report of the 1982 French book market: the ratio of women to men authors is 2:1.

As to why it was only in the 20th century that women began to dominate fiction writing even though they had obviously talked more much before then, it is easy to explain. Writing was regarded as an unbecoming profession for a refined lady of rank, even in Jane Austen's time. Austen always kept a muslin scarf handy and whenever someone approached, she casually tossed it over her manuscript.

Women not only talk more than men but they also speak differently. It would not be in keeping with the spirit of my book to enumerate here all the experiences eminent researchers have acquired working in well-known languages (such as French or Russian) as well as in lesser-known ones (Darkhat, Chukchi, or Koasati). I would just say here that, in general, women's speech tends to be more protracted, more drawn-out. One of the reasons for this is the doubling of vowels. This style of double emphasis invests words with a strong emotional content.

On the other hand, men tend to speak more directly. British and American commercials often feature men. Statements such as "Eat this!... Do this!... Buy this!" sound more unequivocal, more absolute.

Members of the social elite have always regarded emphatic, drawn-out speech with disdain and held it to be unmanly, effeminate. Aiming at a reserved, refined demeanor, they have tended toward compact sounds. Apparently, this is how the French word *beau* (beautiful, handsome) has come to be pronounced to sound approximately like "baw" in order to be regarded as nicely uttered.

Another feature of feminine language is the shift of all consonants towards sibilants /ʃ, s, z/ that gives a slightly affected tone to speech. I think these phonetic changes play the same role as fashion: to emphasize femininity. The male voice is deeper, due to men's anatomical makeup. Today's unisex fashions may not stress gender differences, but I have noticed that young, short-haired girls in their uniforms of jeans and T-shirts instinctively start to twitter at a higher pitch when a guy appears on the horizon.

Another characteristic of female speech is shifting open vowels /a, o, u/ towards more closed vowels. This alternation of open and closed vowels has given rise to doublets.

For some reason, these tend to move from more closed

to open across languages: zigzag,[95] teeny-tiny,[96] knick-knack, bric-a-brac, fiddle-faddle, mishmash, pitter-patter, Tingeltangel,[97] clopin-clopant,[98] cahin-caha,[99] tittle-tattle, and so on.

Feminine speech is characterized by a heightened emotional emphasis at the syntactic level as well. There are more adjectives, and superlatives are more frequently employed. Filler expressions, such as "well," "of course," "still," "yet," "only," "also," "on the contrary," or "I tell you" get greater play. I cannot recommend learning these so-called diluting agents too highly to students of any language.

These are "non-negligible negligibles" because they provide a little space to catch one's breath and to recall the more important elements in the sentence.

My recommendation applies not only to filler words but also to frame expressions: collect them and use them! There was a time when one only heard from women expressions like "The situation is that…" or "What can I say, I…" Lately, they have been cropping up in men's discourse, too. Can we perhaps predict that more feminine turns of phrase are going to gain ground with members of the stronger sex? It would not be surprising, since it is women who pass on language to their children.

To return to my method of language study, what I expect from my Azilian teacher is what I cannot get from either books or the radio. First, I ask the teacher to speak at a slower than average speed so that I can catch as many words as possible from the context; second, I expect him or her to correct my Azilian, mainly on the basis of written assignments that I diligently prepare for each class.

---

95. The Hungarian equivalent is *cikcakk*.
96. The Hungarian equivalent is *csip-csup*.
97. German: cheap nightclub, honky-tonk.
98. French: limping.
99. French: with difficulty.

At first, I write free compositions because it's easier. Often these are disjointed texts, made up of elements not connected with each other, just loose sentences that I use to hang new, just seen/just heard words and grammatical phrases on. From the teacher's corrections I verify whether I grasped their meanings and functions properly. When I reach a higher level of knowledge I begin to translate. At this stage, the text compels me to give up using well-practiced formulas and rely on my translator's discipline, which involves strategies I am not so certain of.

Uncorrected mistakes are very perilous! If one keeps repeating wrong formulas, they take root in the mind and one will be inclined to accept them as authentic. Written translations pinpoint one's errors ruthlessly, while a listening ear might be prone to just glossing over them. I know this from my own translations being "corrected."

For years I chaperoned Chinese guests in Budapest. Heroes' Square would never be left out of the sightseeing program. In the course of these tours, I must have repeated about 50 times that the wreaths nestling against each other at the center of the square were adorning the grave of the *Unknown Soldier* (not "hero" as referred to in the square's name). I translated the expression verbatim. No one ever corrected me; guests are not language teachers. Soon I was given the task of translating a Hungarian tourist brochure into Chinese.

Years later, when I got a copy of the brochure back from Beijing, I discovered that it had been edited. For *Unknown Soldier* the editor had substituted *Nameless Hero*.

I would now like to discuss who one can expect, beyond one's teacher, to correct language mistakes. My experience is that speakers of minor languages will do it. To them, it's still a novelty that their language is being spoken by non-natives or "people from the outer world." They alert one to every single mistake committed, with the zeal of missionaries.

A few years ago I had the opportunity to work with some very cordial and cultivated interpreter colleagues in England. Right at the introductions, I asked them to correct my mistakes. Three weeks later, at our parting, I had to reproach them for not having corrected a single error. Had I not made any mistakes? "Oh, indeed you have," came the reply with a shrug. "But you see, we are so used to it that our ears have developed an automatic error-repairing mechanism. Only corrected forms reach our brains."

My other story is a funny example of the opposite case. A leading politician from a neighboring country was giving a dinner party for several hundred foreign guests. Unfortunately, he delivered the feast-opening toast in his native language which, alas, was not my forte. It is an unforgettably sweet memory for me that he kept stopping me in the middle of my interpreting and telling me that I had committed an error. He would then explain why and how I should have said something. So I, believing him to be sincere about speaking correctly, did not hesitate to miss the opportunity to teach him how he should speak my native language correctly.

There is a great advantage to learning a language through written translations rather than conversation. To speak a foreign language is a matter of practice, and mistakes will be made. Unfortunately, it is difficult for intellectually confident people to accept making mistakes. Therefore they may refrain from speaking. As László Németh[100] says, "Those with real knowledge only want to say what they know." In written translations, this problem does not exist; you do not have to display your knowledge spontaneously, and you usually have the time and resources to avoid making mistakes.

Those who have had the patience to read through my musings on mastering Azilian might find two things lacking in them. Any self-respecting language manual would now

---

100. Hungarian writer of the 20th century.

say something like "I make an effort to familiarize myself with the history, geography, society, politics, and economics of Azilia as thoroughly as possible."

Such study cannot hurt, of course, as it brings us closer to our goal: as comprehensive and precise a knowledge of the language as possible. If I write this with some degree of reluctance, it is because this approach is often abused.

It is much simpler to attend (or give) lectures on the history, politics, economics, etc. of Azilia in one's own language than to torment oneself (or one's students) with the appropriate Azilian vocabulary and grammar needed to learn or teach these subjects.

Years ago, scientists talked of two basic instincts: *Hungertrieb* (hunger instinct) and *Liebestrieb* (love instinct). Philosophers should consider *Reisetrieb* (travel instinct) as well. The desire to travel has developed into a serious motivating force today. I think that World War II and the period of travel restrictions that followed it [for Eastern Europeans] have contributed to this phenomenon. As for the first two *Trieb*s, when their gratification is denied, they too become motivating forces.

So when I hear that "The So-and-So Society" is holding its annual conference in the Azilian capital, Azilville, I do everything in my power to convince my superiors that it is absolutely vital that Hungary be represented at this extraordinary event of global import. Represented by—naturally enough—yours truly.

If my scheme does not lead to success, only a little time was lost (and only among books, trying to find out what on God's green Earth "The So-and-So Society" is all about).

If I succeed in getting permission to travel to Azilville, then the trip's effect on my Azilian may depend on two factors. One is the extent to which I am able to observe and record the natives' speech. The other factor is the extent of my knowledge of Azilian prior to my journey.

It is a grave delusion that merely staying in a foreign

country will allow you to absorb its language. I think people have been misled by the Latin proverb *Saxa loquuntur*, or "Stones talk."

Houses, walls, and buildings do not teach. It may be that they talk, but their speech, alas, is in stone language. It is quite possible to pick up a few colloquial, idiomatic expressions or clever turns of phrase from the locals, but these generally do not amount to any more than what one would have acquired anyway by diligently studying at home.

Neither reminiscing in your native tongue with your émigré compatriots who may now live in Azilia ("Do you remember Alex from sixth grade?"), nor comparative window shopping (or *Schaufensterlecken* in German, meaning "shop window licking") will do anything for your Azilian. Frequent listening to spoken Azilian, however, will. Local papers usually publish information on what museums or galleries offer guided tours. Also, there should be an Azilian branch of the Society for Popular Science Education (or whatever organization you're interested in); they usually offer free lectures to educate the public. Whenever I am abroad, I frequent all these types of events and take copious notes every time.

Going to the movies can help you learn a language. In 1967 I spent three weeks in Moscow, and during that time I went to the movies 17 times. Granted, it was just to the college cinema at Lomonosov University, and a ticket cost only 20 kopecks.[101] But my efforts were noticed: I remember that once the cinema postponed a screening by five minutes just for me, because I was running late.

The ideal solution, of course, is to maintain active relationships with native speakers of one's ilk and interests, with lots of shared activities—especially if these natives are willing to correct your mistakes, and if one is resolved not to get mad at them when they do.

---

101. A kopeck is a coin of the Soviet Union/Russia, worth about 1/100 of a ruble. One kopeck is roughly equal to one cent.

The other factor that decides the impact of a trip on one's knowledge of a language is one's level of mastery at the time of departure. "A" and "F" students will benefit the least from trips. Those who know nothing at the outset will probably return with virgin minds. For those at a very advanced level, improvement will be difficult to detect. The best results will show—given the ideal conditions listed above—at the intermediate level.

*   *   *

My thoughts on language learning are organized into the little compendium below. Heaven forbid that we should call them *Ten Commandments of Language Learning*—let us perhaps call them *Ten Suggestions for Successful Language Learning*.

I.
Spend time tinkering with the language every day. If time is short, try at least to produce a 10-minute monologue. Morning hours are especially valuable in this respect: the early bird catches the word!

II.
If your enthusiasm for studying flags too quickly, don't force the issue but don't stop altogether either. Move to some other form of studying, e.g., instead of reading, listen to the radio; instead of writing a composition, poke about in the dictionary, etc.

III.
Never learn isolated units of speech; rather, learn them in context.

IV.
Write phrases in the margins of your text and use them as "prefabricated elements" in your conversations.

V.

Even a tired brain finds rest and relaxation in quick, impromptu translations of billboard advertisements flashing by, of numbers over doorways, of snippets of overheard conversations, etc., just for its own amusement.

VI.

Memorize only that which has been corrected by a teacher. Do not keep studying sentences you have written that have not been proofread and corrected so mistakes don't take root in your mind. If you study on your own, each sentence you memorize should be kept to a size that precludes the possibility of errors.

VII.

Always memorize idiomatic expressions in the first person singular. For example, "I am only pulling your leg."

VIII.

A foreign language is a castle. It is advisable to besiege it from all directions: newspapers, radio, movies that are not dubbed, technical or scientific papers, textbooks, and the visitor at your neighbor's.

IX.

Do not let the fear of making mistakes keep you from speaking, but do ask your conversation partner to correct you. Most importantly, don't get peeved if he or she actually obliges you—a remote possibility, anyway.

X.

Be firmly convinced that you are a linguistic genius. If the facts demonstrate otherwise, heap blame on the pesky language, your dictionaries, or this book—but not on yourself.

As eight of the biblical Ten Commandments are in the negative, let me now list what *not* to do if you aim to achieve an acceptable level of linguistic mastery within an acceptable time frame.

1.

Do not postpone embarking on learning a new language—or restarting such a study—until the time of a trip abroad. Rather, try to gain access to native speakers who are on a visit to your country and who do not speak your language. They could be relatives or friends. If you accompany them and show them around, they will help you solidify your knowledge of their language out of gratitude; they will enrich your vocabulary and excuse the mistakes you make.

2.

Do not expect the same behavior from your compatriots. Do not practice with them because they will be prone to giving prime time to your errors—or at the very least, they will be inclined to employ meaningful facial gestures—to demonstrate how much better they are at the language than you.

3.

Do not believe that a teacher's instruction, no matter how intense and in-depth it may be, gives you an excuse not to delve into the language on your own. For this reason you should, from the outset, start browsing through illustrated magazines, listening to radio programs and/or prerecorded cassettes, watching movies, etc.

4.

In your browsing, *do not get obsessed* with words you don't know or structures you don't understand. Build comprehension on what you already know. Do not automatically reach for the dictionary if you encounter a word or two you don't recognize. If the expression is important, it will reappear and explain itself; if it is not so important, it is no big loss to gloss over it.

5.

Do not miss writing down your thoughts in the foreign language. Write in simple sentences. For foreign words you can't think of, use one from your own language for the time being.

6.

Do not be deterred from speaking by the fear of making mistakes. The flow of speech creates a chain reaction: the context will lead you to the correct forms.

7.

Do not forget a large number of filler expressions and sentence-launching phrases. It is great when you can break the ice with a few formulas that can help you over the initial embarrassment of beginning a conversation, for example "My French is kind of shaky" or "It's been a while since I spoke Russian," etc.

8.

Do not memorize any linguistic element (expression) outside of its context, partly because a word may have several different meanings. For example, the English word *comforter* may refer to someone who is consoling another, or it can mean a knitted shawl, a quilt or eiderdown, or yet again a baby's pacifier. In addition, it is good, right off the bat, to get used to the practice of leaving the vortex of meanings around the word in your own language alone and reaching out to its kin words in the new language (or to the context you have most frequently encountered it in).

9.

Do not leave newly learned structures or expressions hanging in the air. Fix them in your memory by fitting them into different, new settings: into your sphere of interest, into the reality of your own life.

10.

Do not be shy of learning poems or songs by heart. Good diction is more than the mere articulation of individual sounds. Verses and melodies impose certain constraints; they set which sounds must be long and which must be short. The rhythm inherent in them helps the learner avoid the intonation traps of his native language.

21

Grading Our Linguistic Mastery

≈

A STUDENT can measure his knowledge of a foreign language based on the grades he earns in his classes, at least in theory.

An independent learner, however, will have to do the assessment himself. Since we are biased towards ourselves, I have tried to make my guide to linguistic self-assessment objective.

In this attempt, I have tried to keep in mind the adult who strives to gain a balanced, comprehensive knowledge of a language, rather than a specific skill. The average learner's goal is not to understand the foreign-language publications in his or her field or how to bargain for a sweater; it is most likely just how to speak the language normally.

First, let's look at the grades used in schools.

"A's" and "F's" are the clearest indicators of ability. Students who know nothing will deserve—beyond dispute—an "F." On the other hand, students whose vocabulary in the foreign language seems as broad as in their native tongue and whose speech, pronunciation, and writing only differ from the rules of the language in the ways permitted by it, deserve an "A."

"B's" should be given to those who can read literature in accordance with the author's intention. In addition, you are a "B" student if

- You need a dictionary for at most 20% of the words in a text
- You can improvise a speech on a familiar topic so that native speakers can understand you at first hearing (i.e., without asking back), even if they can perceive you as not being a native speaker by the construction or pronunciation of your sentences
- Your possible gaps in understanding are not usually linguistic-based
- You can compose or translate texts that an editor can make ready for publication quickly and easily.

Those who deserve a "C" understand the essence of texts of average difficulty but not in detail. Likewise, you are a "C" student if

- You may need to ask for information to be repeated on the street or in a store
- You have to construct a message in advance so as to strike the words or uncertain grammatical structures on the imaginary tuning fork first
- You need a dictionary to understand even fairly simple pieces of foreign journalism
- You produce writing that an editor may need to correct or at least verify by consulting sources in the original language.

"D" students are those who can understand texts only after several readings, and then imperfectly; who have difficulty coping with texts even after consulting a dictionary; and who can make themselves understood only with the help of facial expressions, gesticulations, and their partner's goodwill.[102]

The question of the level and self-assessment of language knowledge arises so often that some levels are worth revisiting for better clarity.

A "D" is due those who speak the language at the tourist level. With a handful of sentences, they can ask for a train ticket and look for a room, order lunch, and inquire about the time the evening express leaves. They will figure out from the papers what is on at the movies and they will try to haggle down the price of shoes a bit.

Those who are at the conversational level will receive a better grade, perhaps a "C." It is given to those who can make contacts as a guest or a host; who can give an account of their own country to some extent and can inquire about their partner's; and who can say what they do and will understand the other responding in kind.[103]

There is another level of language ability that I call the EX-IN level. The EX-IN student's passive and active vocabulary is 100% within his or her field. EX-IN students deserve the grade of "B" because they can express their own thoughts in sound grammar and understandable pronun-

---

102. A similar rating system is the Common European Framework of Reference for Languages (CEFR). Dr. Lomb's level A is roughly equal to C1, her B to B2, her C to B1, and her D to A2 or A1.

103. Author's note: I interrupt myself here to give some practical advice to those preparing to go to America. On the train, in the hotel lounge, or at the breakfast table, those sitting next to you will ask you the same questions. First question: "Where are you from?" Second: "What do you do?" Third: "What do you drive?" When I was a novice traveler, I admitted that I usually took the bus. People were so astonished that I changed my answer. I now say, "I don't think you know the make—it's an Ikarus." "Is it a big car?" they would ask. "Is it bigger than a Chevrolet?" "Much bigger!" I would reply with a quick flip of the wrist. [Ikarus is a Hungarian bus manufacturer.]

ciation. Outside their profession, however, they tend to converse quite uncertainly. I recall last summer when I was present at an important international conference led by a Hungarian engineer. He sold several thousand electrical appliances to a foreign partner without ever having to resort to the international language of drawings and diagrams to specify types and sizes.

During a break, we presented the foreign partner with an ice cream, which he ate with apparent delight. "Does it taste you?" the Hungarian engineer asked in English, faithful to the Hungarian form.[104] The poor guest was so frightened that I wanted to comfort him with the words of a song from a film: "It won't eat you, it'll only taste you."[105]

I call the next level the interpreting level. At this level one should know a wide range of vocabulary in different fields, be able to find the key for a variety of pronunciations in an instant, and know how to render messages in the target language as close as possible to the thought expressed in the source language, in both content and style.

Above all these is the native level. Unfortunately, it occurs so rarely that I didn't include it in the childish grading above. The native level is when our countryman is taken for a native-born French, Russian, Brit, etc.; i.e., when he or she starts speaking Hungarian in Paris, Moscow, or London, people will ask in amazement: what is this interesting-sounding language and who put it in your head to learn it?

In this experiment to establish language knowledge levels, I tried to include all pillars—the knowledge of grammar rules, the skill to apply them, and the understanding of

---

104. The Hungarian equivalent is *"Ízlik?"* (Do you like it?)—but its subject is the food and the person who enjoys it is in the dative case, cf. "Does it please you?" in English.
105. Reference to the Hungarian translation of the song "Who's Afraid of the Big Bad Wolf?" in Walt Disney's short film.

heard and written texts. These elements are interconnected. To build a wall, one needs both bricks and mortar.

You can move into an unpainted apartment but you cannot move into one that hasn't had a roof installed by a roofer, or doors hung by a carpenter, or windows glazed by a glazier. And since we are using the house-language analogy, let me reprove my impatient fellow learners by carrying on the metaphor. When building a house, everybody finds it natural that the work begin with a foundation. No one wonders why after many working hours there is nothing to be seen above ground. You may think that you can build without a foundation, but it will only be a castle in the air. When will we finally accept that we must lay a foundation to learn a language, just as we must lay a foundation to build a house?

Each acquired unit—a word or a grammatical form—is also a nail at the same time, on which other words or forms can be hung. Little Pete, mentioned in the Introduction, wanted nails that only jut out. But adults don't always understand, either, that every piece of acquired knowledge builds on something else.

It wouldn't be worth speaking about this self-evident fact if we didn't have so much impatience with language learning. I taught Chinese for half a year at József Attila Free University. One of my students soon dropped out. "Why?" I asked him when I happened to run into him. "Because I had been attending class for a month and I still didn't speak Chinese," he replied.

Returning to levels of language knowledge, let me discuss the most tangible element of the house that is language: words. I've collected a few for a short exercise. Please write the appropriate translation of each in the language of your choice. When finished, you can calculate your grade in lexical knowledge.

I	II
moon	a blow
to buy	to enjoy
free	suddenly
wide	grateful

III	IV
straw	brass
to promote	to browse
rigidly	obstinately
significant	enthusiastic

Score one point for every word in the first group, two points for those in the second, three for those in the third, and four for those in the fourth. Altogether 40 points are possible.

Grading of vocabulary knowledge (in total points):

10 = "D"
20 = "C"
30 = "B"
40 = "A"

Unfortunately, acquired vocabulary is not like a pretty porcelain figure that once you obtain, you can keep enclosed in a display case for the rest of your life. Certainly all of us have experienced how rustily the wheels of our minds creak when we haven't dealt with a foreign language for a while. You used to give yourself a "B" and now, when you take a language out and want to dust it off, it turns out you can hardly reach the "D" level in it.

The idea that unused knowledge fades away is nearly indisputable. Yet I will devote a couple of lines to it because it is not so simple nor unnatural.

First, a certain sedimentation does no harm to language knowledge, just as with wine. I've heard that famous conductors will practice a piece inside out nearly every minute. Then they will put it aside and not touch it before the concert one or two weeks later. They notice that it helps the performance. In language learning, the amount of a language learned while abroad will often not show up until well after arriving home.

Second, one can get tired of a language. I have heard escort interpreters (but also my friends who received foreign guests) complaining of it several times. Upon their guests' arrival, they would speak fluently with them, but during the visit this fluency tended to decrease rather than increase. By the time the moment of departure arrived, the hosts could only spit out *"Bon voyage!"*

The reason for this strange phenomenon is not only that the tourist program (always excessive, due to traditional Hungarian hospitality) tires the brain to death, but the fact that the guests first speak their native languages slowly, clearly, and simply. Later on, they grow so comfortable with the joy of being so well understood in Hungary that they revert back to their accustomed, natural style. And this natural style—the vernacular—has a much looser structure, a more casual construction, and a faster pace. For someone who is not a native speaker, it is not easy to cope with.

A reason why we cannot always believe that "as time passes, you gradually forget the unused language" is that, in the long run, the line showing language knowledge (like that of the growth of the human body) is shaped like a parabola. This image is appropriate because as we proceed towards old age, old memories and the skills acquired in childhood come to the fore, at the expense of those learned later. It is a well-known phenomenon that the grandfather remembers every tiny detail of the Battle of Doberdò, which took place 50 years before. The only thing he forgets is that he recounted it completely half an hour ago.

I heard a story about how the skills we learn early in life stay with us. This is interesting in terms of linguistics as well as of emotion. It comes from a former doyen of our fine arts, Zsigmond Kisfaludi Strobl.

The Hungarian painter Philip de László moved to England in his youth. He married a distinguished English lady and had three sons. He rarely sought out the company of his compatriots, perhaps because the Hungarians who had drifted out of the country after World War I tended to impose themselves on him. On the rare occasions that he did invite over his expatriot artist colleagues, such as our sculptor Mr. Strobl, he apologized and said he could only speak English. He said he had completely forgotten his native tongue.

One night our Mr. Strobl was woken up by a knock at the door. It was an elegant valet, sent by Mrs. de László. She had sent him to collect Strobl because her husband had suddenly taken ill and kept speaking to her in some unknown language. Replies in English were made in vain; he would not respond at all. Strobl hurried to the de László home but, unfortunately, arrived too late. His old friend wasn't able to speak any more, not even in his native tongue, to which he had found his way back after so many decades, in the hour of his death.

22

The Linguistic Gift

≈

UNTIL a new Coloman the Book-lover[106] declares with all of his authority that a gift for languages does not exist, we will hear remarks such as, "He's just good at languages."

No one is "just" good at languages. Success in language learning is determined by a simple equation:

$$\text{Time invested} \times \text{Interestedness} = \text{Result}$$

Is it just playing with words when I write "interestedness" instead of "a gift for languages"? In my opinion, it is not. If language learning were a matter of innate ability, then the same student would tackle different languages with the same efficiency (or inefficiency). However, who hasn't heard (or made) such statements as "Italian is easy, French isn't" or "I have no talent for Slavic languages," etc.?

How can such statements be reconciled with the universality of being "good at languages"?

I have never heard of anyone (otherwise sane in mind) who couldn't speak his or her native language at a level corresponding to their education. However, I have heard of a grandmother who, though having nothing to do with lan-

---

106. A Hungarian king of the 12th century, noted for his decree that "Of witches, since they do not exist, no mention should be made."

guage learning or applied learning of any kind for the past 40 years, learned Spanish at an amazing pace because she was going to visit her grandchild born in South America. I could therefore agree to replace "interestedness" with "motivation" in the above equation.

In language learning, character plays at least as much a role as intellect.

I heard from a swimming coach that how soon children learn to swim depends on how much they trust themselves and the surrounding world. I am convinced that this (self) confidence is the precondition of success in all intellectual endeavors. It may even have a greater role than believed in the least understood human talent: creativity, that is, artistic creation and scientific discovery. In language learning, surviving in the medium of a foreign language demands self-confidence and openness, to which inter- and extrapolation provide invisible swimming ropes.

I don't care for the terms "good at languages" or "not good at languages" because they blithely dismiss any number of complex mental processes. The complaint "I have no talent for languages" usually means that someone can only memorize new words with difficulty, after several tries. The term "good at languages" is given those who imitate the sounds of a foreign language with a parrot-like skill. Other vague appellations exist. The language student who solves written exercises without a mistake is proclaimed a "genius" because she can quickly find her bearings in the morphological and syntactic tangles of a language. The linguaphile who can write in a bold, innovative, and modern style is called a fine writer. The monolingual researcher who, as the result of years-long research, establishes that Old Assyrian loanwords are entirely missing from the various dialects of North Caledonia? Well, he can be called a linguaphile.

A linguaphile—as defined in the Introduction—only needs three skills: a good word memory, the ability to discern sounds, and a logical mind that finds its way in the world of linguistic rules. But approach plays a greater role in the acquisition of vocabulary, good pronunciation, and grammatical perspective than the intangible and indefinable "gift for languages."

It is undeniable that our compatriots from the Great Plain have a more difficult time learning languages than those in Transdanubia or Northern Hungary. What lies behind it, of course, is not that linguistically untalented children come into the world on the mirage-haunted flatland. Instead, it is that those in the pure Hungarian regions hear foreign speech later than those who live in places formerly inhabited by German speakers at the borders of Czechoslovakia or Yugoslavia.

It is an interesting rule that conversation is not absolutely necessary for speech to develop. It is enough in childhood to hear the sounds that don't exist in our mother tongue for the ear to get used to them and for the mouth to be able to reproduce them later. Academics might phrase it as "the foreign-language environment in itself can prevent the articulatory skill from calcification."

Our interpreting team has members who were born and raised abroad as children of Hungarian parents. They came to Hungary more or less as adults after 1945. Although they had never spoken the Hungarian language—only heard it from their parents—they are now perfectly bilingual.

The start or approach, as it is called in English, has a very significant role; it is considerably greater than a "gift for languages" or its absence. Jews have always been famous for being multilingual; those raised in the Kiskunság or Nyírség regions speak foreign languages with just as pure a Hungarian accent as a child from the "civic" Debrecen. Most of the Israeli youth raised in kibbutzim usually speak only Hebrew.

No one can deny the fact that if A and B start learning at the same time, A may reach a level of knowledge in half the time as B does. But if we look closely at each learner, we will likely find out that

- A has more time to devote to dealing with the language than B does
- A is inspired to diligence by a more direct goal than B is
- A uses smarter methods of learning than B does
- A is simply more intelligent than B and this difference in pace would be visible in biology, geology, or any other academic field.

Yet, I believe that there is something to be put into the denominator on the left side of the primitive equation mentioned at the beginning of the chapter. Maybe I would simply call it inhibition:

$$\frac{\text{Time invested} \times \text{Motivation}}{\text{Inhibition}} = \text{Result}$$

Inhibition is shown when the fear of making mistakes prevents you from speaking and also when you are consciously aware that you are transferring the structure of your mother tongue to the new language (or transferring the structure of a previously learned foreign language, which can play the role of the mother tongue at these times).

It is well known that male learners face more inhibitions in speaking than female learners. Istvánné Tálasi aptly wrote in her article "Az idegen nyelvek tanítása" [Foreign language instruction], published in the journal *Köznevelés* [Public education], that educated people speaking a foreign language feel "the tension between their intellectual state of development and the limited opportunities to express themselves in the foreign language." Well, a man usually feels this tension more acutely than a woman.

With women, not only is the tension less, but the desire to communicate is stronger. I can hardly imagine a man playing the role that I did years ago, on a train traveling from Beijing to Pyongyang.

I had been sitting alone and bored for hours when a pretty, smiling little Mongolian woman stepped inside my compartment. Unfortunately, it soon turned out that she didn't speak a word in any other language apart from her mother tongue. My knowledge of Mongolian was restricted to only *bayartai* (goodbye), which I didn't consider suitable to start a conversation.

So we looked sadly at each other for a while. Then my companion took out some provisions from her wicker basket and offered me some. The delicious cookies established my good opinion of Mongolian cuisine more eloquently than any speech. She must have surmised as I turned the pastry in my hand—it resembled our cottage-cheese turnover—that I was racking my brains about how to make it. And that was when the pantomime began. Until the train reached its destination, we exchanged recipes for hours, without exchanging—or being able to exchange—a word. I seem to have correctly "translated" the cooking techniques expressing slicing, breading, thickening, folding, filling, stirring, kneading, cutting, and tenderizing because the meals I learned from this Mongolian woman have since become frequent dishes of my cooking repertoire. And I sometimes imagine with a pleasant feeling that somewhere in Ulanbator a bunch of Mongolian children might be devouring their plates of fried chicken to my health.

The differences in how men and women start to speak a foreign language can be seen in the type of discourse each sex tends to use. Men's thirst for knowledge is just as well-known as women's interest in clothes. However, I must make it clear that after the profession of teaching, it is interpreting that is the most feminine in the world. At a recent conference in Brighton, the interpreters' team consisted of seven women and one man: even the disciplined British couldn't help but laugh.

The public is usually interested in those who are "good at languages" for two reasons. First, because the knowledge of foreign languages is essentially required in everyday life, and second, because language knowledge beyond a certain level leads to such a special world that those outside the gate tend to look in with respectful curiosity. Polyglots have always excited the imagination of monolinguals. Unfortunately, the famous polyglots of the past have not been accurately portrayed in regards to their abilities.

For example, tradition attributes the knowledge of 150 languages to Buddha and it simply records that Muhammad "spoke all languages." According to a local broadcast by Aulus Gellius, Mithridates spoke 25 languages, and it is reported by Plutarch that Cleopatra spoke Coptic, Ethiopian, Hebrew, Arabic, Syriac, Median, and Persian. The queen's multilingualism is not difficult to explain by means of the mathematical formula quoted at the beginning of the chapter: she had plenty of time, since she was relieved of the trouble of housekeeping by her slaves; her uncontrolled political ambitions served as motivation; and her uninhibitedness is eloquently proven by her gallant adventure with Mark Antony. And to stay with the ladies, we can proudly mention the names of Elisabeth, the daughter of Frederick V; Elector Palatine of Pfalz; and Princess Dashkova. It was written about Elisabeth by Descartes himself that she was the only spirit equally well-versed in mathematics and linguistics. Princess Dashkova was elected to be the president of the Russian Academy of Sciences in an age when women were seldom allowed to stray from the kitchen stove.

Even non-linguists know the name Pico della Mirandola. It was reliably recorded about the "admirable Pico" that he spoke 22 languages at the age of 18. His career—like that of many other child prodigies—was short: he died at 31. The pride of the Czech people, John Amos Comenius, not only lay the foundations of modern language instruction but set forth his method in Arabic, Turkish, and Persian—in addition to 12 European languages. We Hungarians can boast of Sándor Kőrösi Csoma: he spoke 18 languages and created the first dictionary of the Tibetan language. In the Russian Lomonosov, we find the rarely co-occurring abilities of a poet, a scientist, and a philologist.

Of the linguists of the past, my favorite is Tom Coryat, the ancestor of all hippies. This delightful tramp lived at the end of the 16th century and never worked. His official trade was vagrancy: he set off at the age of 16 and walked 2000 miles, acquiring 14 languages in the process. According to his pledge, he never rode a cart nor changed his shoes—an example worth bearing in mind for our comfort-loving youth and also for our shoe manufacturing. By the way, he hung his much-weathered shoes on a church gate in the English village of Odcombe when he returned from wandering; the tatters are said to be still visible today.

It is, however, undoubtedly the Italian cardinal Mezzofanti who takes the top honors. He deserves discussing a bit longer not only because of his extraordinary method and unsurpassable results, but because he was a great friend of Hungarian.

When Mezzofanti's name arises, it is commonly disputed how many languages he actually spoke. Some scholars mention 100; he himself professed in 1839 that "I speak 50 languages and Bolognese." He admitted "70 or 80 and some dialects" in 1846. And he learned them all by never leaving the borders of Italy. In fact he claimed he didn't even go more than 25 miles away from his hometown, Bologna.[107]

He was born the umpteenth child of poor working-class parents. When it was discovered before he entered school that he could flawlessly memorize and reproduce the Latin words he heard on the street, he was given to the only intellectual career then open to the poor—theology.

---

107. Actually, he traveled 250 miles to Rome, but it may have happened after he had acquired his languages.

The various wars provided ample opportunity for him to get acquainted with diverse languages as a confessor of the injured in the hospital of Bologna. His method was more or less the same as Kossuth's, except that it wasn't a Shakespeare play that he used as a starting point but the Creed, the Hail Mary, and the Lord's Prayer. He told dying soldiers to speak these religious recitations in their mother tongues, and that is how he learned the word-forming, sentence-constructing, and pronunciation rules of their languages.

The young priest soon gained worldwide fame and the church and lay notabilities who passed through Bologna didn't miss paying him a visit. With childlike modesty he attributed all his results to two factors—his energy and persistence. Foreigners assembled in the chamber "Accademia Poliglotta di Propaganda"[108] to pay him tribute. He answered their questions one by one—always in their language. Eyewitnesses note that he switched from one language to another without any hitch or transition and that he wrote epigrams or exhortations for visitors at their request.

According to the historical record, Mezzofanti learned as many as four Hungarian dialects from displaced soldiers. Whether a "pesthi" dialect actually existed and whether the "Eperies" dialect was in fact some variant of Slovak is difficult to determine 150 years later. But it is more interesting to cite what Cardinal Mezzofanti thought about Hungarian:

> "Do you know what language I place before all others, next to Greek and Italian, for constructive capability and rhythmical harmoniousness?— The Hungarian. I know some pieces of the later poets of Hungary, and their melody took me completely by surprise. Mark its future history, and you will see in it a sudden outburst of poetic

---

108. It was part of the Sacred Congregation for the Propagation of the Faith (Sacra Congregatio de Propaganda Fide), called Congregation for the Evangelization of Peoples since 1982.

genius, which will fully confirm my prediction. The Hungarians themselves do not seem to be aware of what a treasure they have in their language." (Quoted by Watts, "Transactions of the Phyl. Society," 1855)[109]

How could anyone not like this kind scholar?

Mezzofanti once wrote in the notebook of one of his admirers that "Anyone who can comprehend, analyze, judge, and memorize the essence of languages can equal my achievement."

---

109. The actual source of this quote is *The Life of Cardinal Mezzofanti* by C. W. Russell (1863). (See http://how-to-learn-any-language.com/e/mezzofanti/index.html)

23

Language Careers

≈

TO PREVENT depression, psychologists advise us to find a hobby. G. B. Shaw says as much in *Pygmalion*: "Happy is the man who can make a living by his hobby!"

Admitting bias, I believe that those who choose languages as their obsession never really feel depression. In fact linguaphiles may achieve a spiritual balance if they can make a living off of languages. How can a linguaphile make a living off of his or her passion? There are three occupations—international business, catering, and tourism—that generally require practical foreign language skills, and three—language instruction, translation, and interpreting—that require formal foreign language education. It is the problems of the latter three that I will discuss in this chapter.

Our public education system is guilty of a grave omission in preparing students for language careers. Only for language teaching does it offer a systematic training program and thus official qualifications. We—translators and interpreters—have called attention to this problem several times at meetings, in professional communications, in statistical reports, and in the daily newspaper. It is clear to us that certifiable training in the art of translation and interpreting is not only demanded by the young, but also by the translating and interpreting profession.[110]

The financial, administrative, and pedagogical aspects of this question are outside the scope of this book. I would like only to point out that although the main requirement of these three careers is identical—a high-level knowledge of a language—the careers are actually very different.

For teaching, language knowledge is worth nothing unless coupled with pedagogical and psychological knowledge and a sincere sense of vocation. Likewise, a successful language educator will not automatically succeed in the interpreting booth. And I could cite examples to show how an outstanding interpreter produced a poor written translation, or how a translator with enormous experience was still looking for the predicate of a speaker's first sentence long after the speaker had bowed and sat down.

It would be easy to argue that some didn't succeed because of lack of practice. Experience, however, shows something else: it is not a matter of practice but of personality that determines which of the three language careers one can succeed in.

The most important factor that differentiates these three arts—and which is decisive in their success or failure—is time.

Only those who are not introverted and not deterred from being in the limelight should become teachers or interpreters. After actors, it is teachers who are most on stage. The only difference is that an actor can study all the details of his or her performance in advance and then play the role for weeks, months, or in lucky cases years. A teacher and an interpreter, on the other hand, can face variables on stage. But while a teacher can usually control his environment, an

---

110. This training has been in Hungary since the second edition of this book. The Department of Translation and Interpreting, formerly known as the Training Centre for Translation and Interpreting, was established in 1973 (source: http://www.elteftt.hu/index_English.asp?id=2).

interpreter's life is nothing but unpredictability.

The proposition advocated by Kosztolányi ("speaking a foreign language always means a compromise") applies more to interpreters than to teachers. It is actually more appropriate to require educators to be infallible.

When Russian first began being taught in Hungary, it wasn't unusual for a teacher to rack his brain along with his pupils about the meaning of a difficult sentence. This partisan period, however, is of the past. Today a teacher's responsibilities and duties are usually outlined well in advance; hence there is no place for uncertainty.

An introverted and hesitant individual who is prone to self-criticism may only be suitable for translation work. This job requires a deeper knowledge of language than teaching because, in order to make a decent living, translators must work with all manner of texts; even the most highly skilled practitioners, the literary translators, can't afford to specialize in a single subject, writer, or style. Technical translators also must frequently translate a wide variety of texts.

I recall an incident where an American guest at an international congress took the trouble to come to my interpreting booth and tell me that I had chosen the wrong term for a concept. He then provided the correct expression. I thanked him for his help and then asked him to tell me the translation of another expression which I was uncertain of. "Ah, I don't know that," he replied. "I am only an expert in the polymerization of *solid* bodies; I am not familiar at all with the one occurring in the *liquid* phase!"

How can a literary and a technical translator do their diverse jobs? By being a universal genius or a polymath? Not likely. Fortunately, they are treated mercifully by the tyrant of our trade: time. They can search for better and better solutions according to their liking and conscience; they can consult dictionaries and experts.

Interpreters, however, tacitly agree to compromise from the start. Only those who don't suffer from perfectionism should choose this career. An interpreter's job is an eternal compromise between the ideal of "I would like it perfect" and the reality of "that is what my time allowed." This is the only field where—due to the tyranny of time—the French saying cannot apply: *le bon est l'ennemi du meilleur* (good is the enemy of better). He who cannot accept the good instead of the better will not reap many laurels in this most interesting of language careers. Let me devote a special chapter to it.

24

The Interpreting Career

≈

> "And the Lord said, 'Behold, they are one people,
> and they have all one language; and this is only
> the beginning of what they will do; and noth-
> ing that they propose to do will now be impos-
> sible for them. Come, let us go down, and there
> confuse their language, that they may not under-
> stand one another's speech.'"
>
> Genesis 11.1–2

AND SO it was in Babel, and all the earth. Yet I am
certain that within hours of hearing babble, people found
interpreters to tell them what certain angry sounds directed
at them meant. The interpreting profession was born.

To my knowledge there are no firsthand accounts by or
about the first practitioners of our trade. Pliny the Elder (A.D.
23–79) may be the first to mention interpreters: he writes
that there were as many as 130 working in Dioscurias[111] on
a regular basis.

The fall of the Roman Empire seems to have buried the
profession under its ruins. We know that some synods in
the early Middle Ages argued in Latin, others in Greek, and

---

111. Today: Sukhumi in Abkhazia, Georgia.

187

yet others in Hebrew: they didn't understand each other and therefore didn't convince each other, either.

Interpreters played a role at the onset of trade relations between the East and the West. Foreign-trade "operators" with a knowledge of Western languages, called dragomans, appeared at the courts of sultans.

Regarding the origin of *dragoman*, I have found two explanations. The first is that it comes from the Old Arabic *tarjuman* (intermediary); the second, from the Anglo-Saxon *druggerman* (drudge, coolie). After a long day of simultaneous interpreting, I always favor the latter hypothesis.

In Naima's *Annals of the Turkish Empire,* there is only one dragoman specifically mentioned. He spoke 14 languages. We can be proud of him: he was a Hungarian.

Today it is strange to hear that the reason why the interpreter's trade was on the rise in the Renaissance was because the dukes of Venice and Genoa didn't understand each other. Like painters and sculptors, these ancient representatives of our trade enjoyed the favor of patrons and enhanced the splendor of their households.

It was around the beginning of the 19th century when artists were liberated from their aristocratic patrons; interpreters became independent a century later. Interpreting as an occupation is the eighth sister of the *septem artes liberales*, the seven liberal arts.

It took a great thunder to come about. Our profession gained importance when humankind, still half-blind from the terror of World War II, started to grope for the paths of coexistence.

Until that time, diplomacy had been conducted solely by diplomats, who had their common language: French. It is food for thought that at the Congress of Vienna assembled after the fall of Napoleon in 1815, it was in French that the representatives of the Holy Alliance discussed the methods of eclipsing the French language and culture.

In 1945, nations began to look for cooperation in so

many political, commercial, economic, cultural, and scientific areas that the situation radically changed. It was not always possible for governments or businesses to expect interpreters to have political, commercial, and economic knowledge (to give just three examples) as well as language knowledge. Furthermore, the demand for interpreters could no longer be satisfied by those simply raised bi- or trilingually. A systematic training of interpreters began in various schools, which number perhaps 30–40 worldwide today.

It is difficult to quote an exact figure because there is no large city in the West without a school that trains interpreters. Worldwide, interpreting is among the better-paid professions.

The general public thinks of interpreters as being members of a uniform profession, in the same way that they believed peasants to be of a uniform class until the liberation of 1945. Escort, negotiation, and conference interpreters are distinct occupations. They each have different requirements, different tasks, and different levels of remuneration.

Escort interpreters are employed on a regular basis by tour groups and on an occasional basis by social organizations, whose responsibilities include the entertainment of foreigners. Only those who are specially certified can be a tour guide. Obtaining the certificate is linked to an examination, and the examination to completing a course. Apart from language knowledge and political cognizance, potential escort interpreters have to give evidence that they know history, literature, and art history. The saying that everyone in contact with a foreigner is also an ambassador of his or her homeland particularly holds for this category of interpreter, through whose eyes the guest can see our country and through whose words they are acquainted with it. It is a human trait that we judge whole peoples and even whole continents through those with whom we have had a personal relationship. Thus it is no wonder that we have high personal, professional, political, and moral requirements for escort interpreters. Unfortunately, their remuneration is painfully low for the important work they do.

Negotiation interpreters function within the framework of a company, an institute, or a corporation. It is the detailed and thorough knowledge of the field that matters in this job, apart from good language knowledge. Translation is usually done consecutively, that is, after a part of the message is spoken. Besides good language knowledge, this job makes a special demand on interpreters: a good memory. There is a noting system that plays a great role in the curricula of interpreters' schools (interestingly, shorthand is completely unsuitable for this purpose), which enables memory to be aided to some extent.

This high-level but time-consuming method is more and more replaced at international meetings by synchronous or *simultaneous interpreting*. Simultaneous interpreting is when the interpreter listens to the discussion or lecture in an acoustically isolated booth, through headphones, and translates what is being said into the target language. The interpreter speaks into a microphone, not to a person.

Simultaneous interpreting is one of the most modern and intellectually interesting professions. Everyone accepts the former claim; many debate the latter. Doubters claim that interpreting is not an intellectual function but just its opposite.

It is undeniable that the transmitted facts don't always have to penetrate into the interpreters' minds. Truly experienced interpreters can even consciously switch off part of their minds from work. But the job is still no less intellectually strenuous: a simultaneous interpreter needs a rest after 15–20 minutes. This is why there is always a pair of interpreters working in a booth.

What makes this job so difficult? What explains why there are 50–60 really good negotiation interpreters in Hungary but only a few simultaneous interpreters?

I have three reasons.

First, although simultaneous interpreters essentially don't do anything different from what those who are starting to speak a foreign language do—interpret from the source language into the target language—they interpret ready-made messages rather than their own thoughts. That is why it is so difficult (though, peversely, why some say it is not a true intellectual activity.)

Second, simultaneous interpreting is so new that no one has tried to analyze it from a linguistic point of view and there is no significant research on it either in Hungary or abroad.[112]

And third, simultaneous interpreting is the manifestation of the highest level of achievement in a foreign language.

Simultaneous interpreting is a type of thought transmission that has built-in difficulties that can't be overcome solely by linguistic or professional knowledge. More important than both is to have the skill so that the intellect can break out of the sphere of the source language and start revolving in the orbit of the target language, from one matrix of forms to another.

Why is this task more difficult during simultaneous interpreting than in the course of everyday talking? Because in simple conversations (and especially in written translations) we have some time to think over what we have to say and to check the correctness of the new form by "striking the tuning fork" mentioned earlier. We have time to construct our message even in consecutive interpreting because the person being translated gives us pre-constructed units, i.e., finished sentences.

Unfortunately, in simultaneous interpreting we deal with many semi-finished sentences. "When he is dissected after his death," a disrespectful interpreter said of a foreign dignitary, "a million predicates will be found in his stom-

---

112. A dated claim.

ach: those he swallowed in the past decades without saying them." In the hope that some readers of this book are current and would-be speakers (lecturers, broadcasters, reporters), let me take the opportunity to forward two requests to you. First, when you improvise, don't use the stiltedness of written style, fairly widespread in Hungary. You will become entangled in it and you won't be able to finish your first sentence. Second, if you have carefully scripted your high-falutin message beforehand at home, please give us a copy. When a speaker recites intricately polished, long sentences from his script and we have to improvise, then a wrestling match between speaker and interpreter ensues. All we can do is wrestle in the Greco-Roman style while the speaker does so in a "catch-as-catch-can" way. In this struggle, we are always defeated.

Let me say once again that the reason why simultaneous interpreting is more difficult than spontaneous talking is that the interpreter has only split seconds at his disposal for thinking. In fact the interpreter is often in the red: he has to guess in advance how what he is translating right now will sound in a couple of seconds.

Let me support this statement with a specific example. Let's suppose that the sentence to be translated is this:

> "Water-soluble salts are **not** suitable for the production of this medicine, mostly used in veterinary practice."

As in every communication, there is a keyword—a new element—that expresses the essence of the message. It may be something that neither the interpreter nor even experts know yet; it may be something destined to be taught in universities from this point on. In this sentence, the essence that cannot be foreseen—the new element—is the word

not. It is in the fourth position.[113]

However, what happens if we translate the following sentence as it is being spoken:

"Wasserlösliche Salze eignen sich zur Herstellung dieses, hauptsächlich in der Veterinärmedizin verwendeten Medikaments **nicht**."

The essence of the message, the reason why the speaker is speaking it and why the audience is listening, is the word **nicht**. It is in the 14th position.

The easiest solution would be for the interpreter to wait for the speaker to say the keyword **nicht** before he or she starts interpreting. The reason why the interpreter cannot always do this in practice is because the information preceding the keyword may be complex enough that it needs to be spoken immediately in order not to be missed. Anyway, only the speaker is allowed to stop. ("A profound mind, searching for the most suitable form to express his thoughts!") If it is the interpreter who falls silent, then the sudden silence will awake even the delegates napping peacefully in their headphones. ("There are amateurs sitting in the booths; they don't know the terms.")

So if the keyword keeps you waiting, do not let dead silence reveal the difficulties of your task. This is where you may need to use the filler expressions mentioned in the chapter on vocabulary. That list can be supplemented with others. It is worth noting that forms from the formal language of lectures and speeches can provide more of the necessary lubricants than forms from everyday conversation.

The word order of different languages is not the same. The reason why it is difficult to translate from German is

---

113. It is the same in the original Hungarian example: "Vízben oldható sók **nem** alkalmasak ennek a gyógyszernek az előállítására, amelyet főleg az állatorvosi gyakorlatban használnak."

that the language likes "formations" as long as possible. The subordinate clauses endlessly linked to each other are expressed in English as "a box in a box in a box" and in German itself as *Schachtelsätze* or box sentences. But while this style of embedded clauses is mostly a matter of fashion in German, in Japanese it is the only grammatical possibility. This language doesn't know the system of subordinate clauses. A poor interpreter will sweat until he or she manages to handle a sentence like, "My friend related yesterday his meeting with a little girl desperately crying for not being able to buy a book having lost the honorable money received from her mother to buy the book."

(The word "honorable" is not long in Japanese but it is indispensable. It can never be omitted—especially by women—in connection with money, business cards, messages, and a number of other things. Let's not be surprised: in this polite country even a doll is called *ningyō-san* [human-shaped gentleman]).

Interpreting is teamwork. We not only expect our partner in the booth to relieve us when we are tired, but also to help us with words that slip our minds. If he is not present or if he doesn't know the word either, remember what I have said about synonyms, filler expressions, circumlocution, etc.

Let me mention another factor when describing the beauties and difficulties of our job. International meetings are forms of technical, economic, and scientific cooperation. There are several international organizations like the UN, the European Economic Community,[114] the International Organization for Standardization, and the General Agreement on Tariffs and Trade that develop their uniform principles year by year at conferences. The participants have known each other for years. We know, for example, that

---

114. Renamed "European Community" in 1992, the first pillar of today's European Union.

while Mr. Craig insists on the Ultra-Turrax apparatus for the homogenization of cooked meat in order to determine its phosphatase activity, Herr Schulze will exclusively accept the Nelco apparatus for this purpose. The only problem is that the last conference took place maybe in Barcelona and the preceding one, say, in Leningrad.[115] So the poor Hungarian interpreter, with sentences of the discussion flitting around his or her head as fast as lightning, is still wondering what on earth phosphatase activity may be.

We are motivated to overcome these difficulties by our love of the profession. We have only one request to those whom we serve with so much endeavor: let them not regard us as a necessary evil.

Today it is not the representatives of the privileged classes with knowledge of French who meet at international forums, but experts of science, activism, and technology. Requirements for them are numerous and diverse: comprehensive technical knowledge and an instinctive knowledge of mankind, strength of principles, and diplomatic tact. It can't always be expected that they will speak foreign languages at the high level required at improvised discussions. If we, interpreters, relieve them of this burden, we will exempt them of the necessity of speaking a broken language, which shatters authority. "I would rather keep silent perfectly than speak imperfectly," a clever minister of ours once said.

Our foreign partners appear to take the same position, though they are generally familiar enough with English to use it. However, they usually have an interpreter present just in case. Once, however, a visit almost failed in spite of an interpreter being present.

While we were at a meeting in a foreign country, our host could not go beyond the level of "How do you do?" He stuttered with regret that there was only one person in his small office who could speak a foreign language, and that

---

115. Renamed St. Petersburg in 1991.

language was Chinese.

I shrugged with an offhand gesture: what is it to me? For I knew the language.

The gentleman in question soon appeared. He had a huge wart on his chubby face with three long hairs jutting out of it. Apparently they don't cut them off because they bring luck. Even when we took our seats, he was stroking them proudly and conceitedly.

At his first words, however, my obligatory polite smile froze on my lips. I had no right to be so confident: I didn't understand a word of his Chinese and he hardly any of mine. He spoke a clear Cantonese dialect, something perfectly different from what I had been taught at the university in Budapest.

It wasn't quite pleasant for me but he completely paled. If it turned out that he couldn't understand the official Chinese, Mandarin, he would lose face, and a more serious thing cannot happen to an Eastern person. He tried the Hakka dialect; I didn't understand it any better than Cantonese. After a few minutes' agony, the solution occurred to us at last. Chinese written characters are the same in all dialects, so we quickly wrote down our messages and passed them to each other under the desk. I cheated just as I had done decades before in my secondary-school math classes in Pécs. We had luck: we didn't go beyond the obligatory polite phrases. We drank the usual jasmine tea and withdrew from the room amidst deep bows and with undamaged prestige. Yet, I still break out in a sweat whenever I recall the incident.

Let me relate two other stories about linguistic difficulties. I heard one from Peter Ustinov, which I like to tell to all my Esperanto-loving friends.

Ustinov, the British writer, director, and actor of Russian ancestry, was also an ambassador for a while. His station was in a Western capital. When he arrived, he visited his fellow diplomats one after the other.

When he called on the Chinese diplomat, he was led

into a large, elegant room in which the short Asian diplomat was almost lost. After the diplomat offered him a chair and then took a seat himself, he rang a bell. An even smaller man entered, apparently the diplomat's Western secretary and interpreter. The diplomat told him something, but the secretary/interpreter didn't understand him and said so. The diplomat repeated himself, but the poor man still didn't understand. After several more failed exchanges, the diplomat furiously pulled out a paper and a pen, drew something, and handed it to his subordinate. There was a teacup on the paper.

The suffering protagonist of my second story is me. At the very beginning of my interpreting career, a Japanese guest arrived in Hungary. I prepared with great excitement for the first official event: a ceremonial visit to a leading statesman of ours.

I comforted myself with the thought that during the visit, planned to last 10 minutes, a very in-depth professional negotiation couldn't be expected to transpire. But just in case, I wrote out two pages of terms that I thought were likely to arise. "Fortification of relations." "Increase in foreign trade turnover." "An improved level of acquaintance with each other's culture." And so on and so forth.

The Japanese guest and I went to meet the Hungarian statesman. As we opened his upholstered door, he hurried to meet us. As soon as he sat us down, he mentioned that he had just read that our movie *Merry-Go-Round*[116] had been screened in Japan. I paled. "Merry-go-round" was not included in the standard vocabulary of diplomacy. I had no idea how it was expressed in Japanese. I tried circumlocution for a while. I didn't succeed. Then I tried to draw it: the guest turned the paper around and about, then stated that his eyesight had been failing recently. Eventually, I started running

---

116. The movie, shown at the Cannes Film Festival in 1956, is considered a classic of Hungarian cinema.

around the room in a wavy line, with enthusiastic screams now and then. At this point, the host interrupted, remarking that indeed, the great heat would sometimes drive him crazy too. Yet, it must have turned a light on in our Japanese guest's mind because he suddenly struck his forehead: "Ah, merry-go-round!" It turned out that there was no Japanese term for it: they simply use the English term.

25

Reminiscences from My Travels

≈

AN INTERPRETER'S life is full of instructive, elevating, delightful, and thought-provoking experiences. I have found it tiring but never boring.

I have often thanked the invisible hand that led me to learn foreign languages. Aside from the joy of learning them, how many wonderful experiences I owe to the fact that they opened the door to the world for me! They are the reason I have traveled to practically every European country, most in Asia, and many in Africa and North and Central America. I've ventured to extreme locales as well; in May 1969, I wasn't far from the Tropic of Cancer, and in August of the same year, I crossed the Arctic Circle in the Finnish city of Rovaniemi.

I often think of a short story by Jókai in relation to language learning and salvation. The story's protagonist is a young Russian girl held captive in the tsar's lead mines in Siberia. One day she manages to escape with some of her companions. The little group wanders down overgrown paths hungry and thirsty, hoping to find someone to beg food from, when in the depths of the forest they come across a desolate tomb with an inscription in Volapük.[117] The little girl kneels down before it, reads it, and cries out: *"Dán olik pükatidel volapüken!"*[118] (O thank you, my old Volapük teacher!) The others kneel down too, believing their companion has discovered a new, more merciful god. However, the girl is only thanking her former teacher: the Volapük inscription on the tomb tells the way out of the taiga. The little group is saved.

If I live to see the day when a linguist pronounces glottal sounds in a bilabial way—e.g., *hamu* as *mamu*[119]—it will be a memory that will warm my heart. But let me relate some heart-warming memories that actually happened.

When I am asked about memorable experiences, I usually talk about three particular meetings. I will relate them here in chronological order.

In 1959, I was in Hanoi with a Hungarian delegation. One item on the program was a meeting with Phạm Văn Đồng, Prime Minister of North Vietnam. Ten minutes were estimated for the reception; I thought the usual "protocol generalities" would arise. It was not the case. The Prime Minister called upon each member of the delegation by name, one by one, to ask him or her what they saw of value in Vietnam or what they saw was lacking. The meeting extended to an hour; all the Prime Minister did was listen and ask questions. Those 60 minutes were a historic lesson for all of us.

---

117. Volapük was a language created in 1880 by Johann Martin Schleyer, a Roman Catholic priest in Baden, Germany. Schleyer proclaimed that God had come to him in a dream and asked him to create a universal human language. Volapük became popular all over Europe. By 1889 there were hundreds of Volapük clubs and textbooks.
118. This is Jókai's version but the correct form may be *"Danob oli, o pükatidel volapüka!"*
119. Reference to a humorous Hungarian saying about very old age. *Hamu* means ash.

The other meeting was not about current events but about the past, indeed the most distant past: the appearance of life on Earth. Two acknowledged experts of this question are the Soviet professor Oparin and the Irish professor Bernal. The two scientists met in Hungary; I had the honor of being their interpreter. I not only admired their stunning knowledge but also their sense of humor. However, on any particular question, Bernal couldn't possibly accept the argument of his partner.

"Then let's leave it at the world being created by God!" he exclaimed.

"Or that there is no life on Earth!" retorted professor Oparin.

When saying goodbye, I asked them if I might have a request. "Of course, go ahead!" they encouraged me. I turned to professor Bernal, who I knew was an expert in machine translation, and asked him not to hurry with perfecting these apparatuses because in that case we, interpreters, would be out of work. He comforted me by laughing and saying that machine translation would not be able to replace humans for a long time. To prove this, he related the following story.

Once he and his team used a computer to translate an English expression—"Out of sight, out of mind"—into German. But a computer is only logical; thus it translated the first part as "outside the sight" and the second as "outside the mind." What is out of sight is invisible and one who is out of mind is insane. That is why when the German result was entered back into the computer for confirmation, the computer produced "invisible idiot."

My third experience concerned not the present or the past but the future. It involved Dr. Christian Barnard, a pioneer in heart transplants, who was speaking with eloquence and a convincing optimism about the prospects of organ transplants. Let me note a kind human trait about him. He had only two days in Budapest but was cheerful when, in good Hungarian style, we tried to extract at least two weeks' worth of speeches, meetings, interviews, and statements from him.

At one point he came to a lecture five minutes early. There were at least 20 physicians, radio people, journalists, and photographers waiting for him in the lobby. He glanced around somewhat frightened; then he caught sight of an elderly lady silently weeping in a corner. "What is that lady's problem?" he asked. It turned out that the woman had brought her 12-year-old son to Budapest for a serious heart operation and she wanted to see the great specialist. Professor Barnard spent the remaining free minutes comforting her.

Anyway, Dr. Barnard withstood the rush of journalists well; the only time he became embarrassed was when he was asked to write a greeting. "Oh, how do you spell *Hungarian?*" he asked desperately. "I was absent from school the day spelling was taught."

Many may wonder why the interpreting profession is not more competitive if it offers so many interesting experiences. The explanation is, I think, because it requires an unusual combination of skills: the ability to associate ideas as fast as lightning, an imperturbable calmness, a good nervous system, and, most of all, a never-ceasing readiness to study. An interpreter takes exams 30–40 times a year in front of an international panel, in such disparate subjects as the diagnosis of brain tumors, the application of mathematical models in agricultural planning, the mechanical features of thermoplastic materials, and/or the future direction of aleatoric music.

It often turns out in the interpreting booth that the tasks are bigger than what you imagined. Let me relate a personal experience in connection with this.

When I was a novice interpreter, I once went into the French booth with chattering teeth. It felt good that a self-confident gentleman with a resolute appearance was perched beside me. He was sent by the organizers, he told me, to help me if I got stuck and correct me if I made a mistake. I could hardly spit out the first sentence—*"Nous saluons les délégués venus de tous les coins du monde"* (Welcome to the delegates who arrived from all corners of the world)—when he covered the microphone and warned me: "Comrade, you can't say that. The Earth is round, the world has no corners!"

After two or three such "corrections," I offered to change places with him: he could take over the translation since he was obviously much better than me. "Very well," he nodded. "I'll only go to the organizers and tell them about the change." He left—and he hasn't come back since, although 20–25 years have passed.

The introductory, welcoming salutations of meetings are usually rather schematic and they provide some pleasant warm-up for the real tasks. Yet, my most embarrassing experience involves them. We were in Stockholm at an international conference and the Russian booth was assigned to me. The meeting was opened by the president and he welcomed first the brother of the Swedish king, present at the conference. The phrases "Your Royal Highness"… *"Königliche Hoheit"*… *"Votre Altesse Royale"* were all said in the other booths but I was stuck in silent anguish about how to say "royal highness" in Russian.[120]

Sometimes it is the topic, sometimes the speaker, that causes awkward moments in interpreting. The case of a Hungarian ornithologist in Germany is an example of the former. He was invited to give a lecture in his field and a Hungarian student who studied there was provided for him as an interpreter. The first picture was shown and the ornithologist began: "This is a hoopoe with perching legs and a

---

120. *Ваше королевское величество.*

double-feathered crest that can be made erected or decum-
bent." Utter silence followed. Then the interpreter started to
speak: *"Vogel!"* (bird)

The other story happened to me, unfortunately. I was
hired to interpret into Japanese for the first time in my life.
The Hungarian hosts and I were waiting at the Ferihegy
airport. Our leader was a widely popular, old politician
known for his flowery style, but my knowledge of Japanese
didn't permit me to say much more than "Japanese is good,
Hungarian is good, long live!" However, the first sentence
I was supposed to translate into Japanese (and with which
I was supposed to launch my career) went like this: "The
black army of weed-scatterers will in vain try to obscure
the unclouded sky of the friendship between Japanese and
Hungarian peoples!"

Sometimes it is neither the topic nor the speaker but the
language itself that causes the interpreter to suffer. We have
already touched upon a feature of German: it can postpone
the predicate to the end of the sentence. A classic anecdote
about this comes from Mark Twain. He was in Germany for
a visit and wished to see a historical play. But since he didn't
speak German, he had an interpreter sit beside him. The
spotlights went on, the curtain was raised, the protagonist
appeared, and his eloquent diction was heard for minutes
but the interpreter still didn't say a word.

"Why don't you interpret?" Mark Twain nudged him.

"Hush," our colleague whispered. "The predicate is only
coming now!"

One of the best Hungarian interpreters had a similar experience. The speaker she was supposed to translate for grew
entangled in his own flowery speech and our poor colleague
tried to hang on to the lifejacket of some verb. "Why don't
you translate?" he asked her. "I'm waiting for the predicate,"
she replied. "Don't translate the predicate," he snapped at
her. "Translate what *I* say!"

The next program item is not recommended for our readers under 12.

I got a phone call from a government minister: a Japanese guest of outstanding stature had arrived and I should immediately go to the lounge of hotel X and try to entertain him until the ministry officials arrived. I hurried there. I was received by a young, skinny, and humble man. I started the prescribed entertainment: I asked him what the purpose of his visit to Hungary was. He answered with a Japanese word that I didn't understand. I asked him to write down its hieroglyph but he declined, finding it too complicated. But it occurred to him that the English translation of the term was written for him somewhere. He pulled out a slip of paper from his pocket, which contained only one word:

Sexing

Then he told me that the Hungarian state paid him very well for this activity on a daily basis.

I got embarrassed. Is it possible that this "activity" occurs to every man when he goes abroad? And what kind of man can admit to it so straightforwardly and, what's more, enjoy such generous financial support from our state to do it?

I was given an explanation by the arriving ministry officials. Our Japanese guest was an expert in distinguishing day-old chicks by sex. His task was to separate future roosters, worthless for further breeding, to save cage space and chicken feed. Interestingly, it is only the Japanese who are experts at this.

Long pages could be filled with the blunders—slips of the tongue—made by interpreters. I will cite only one of them. At a congress of film critics, the interpreter accidentally said *fogalmazás* (composition [wording]) instead of *fogamzás* (conception [fertilization]). "Now I know why Hungarian movie scripts are so bad sometimes," her relief partner remarked. "Scriptwriters use preventive devices for composition."[121]

I am also grateful to my profession because it flew me across continents split up by country borders. My travel experiences don't belong in the framework of this book and they would be disappointing anyway because I never looked for or found national differences in the various places of the world, only common features—eternal human nature.[122]

The most fascinating sight I have seen in my travels is perhaps the *Pithecanthropus pekinensis* of the Chinese museum. This huge ape is still perfectly an animal but at the same time is halfway human. I felt as if a distorting mirror of all humankind were held up for me to see. I couldn't get away from its influence for days. It is wonderful as an exhibition as well: the showcase is padded with faceted mirrors so wherever beholders are standing, they can see the ape from all sides—and themselves.

At the time of our visit, there was a group of Korean schoolgirls in the museum. Well, it wasn't until the teenagers—each and every one—arranged the red ribbons in their plaits in the mirror of the showcase that they looked at the exciting sight and discussed it in their twittering voices.

The venue of my other great experience was the Siberian taiga. We set off on an all-day excursion to Lake Baikal. A well-known, ominous sight aroused me from the spell of the landscape: a palm-sized run in my stocking. "Don't worry," our guide comforted me. "We will buy a pair in the nearest shop." We did find a shop in a tiny kolkhoz[123] village.

---

121. A word-play: *fogamzásgátló* means contraceptive and its made-up version *fogalmazásgátló* would refer to a device that prevents composition skills.

122. Dr. Lomb's travel experiences are documented in *Egy tolmács a világ körül* [An interpreter around the world].

123. A form of collective farming in the Soviet Union.

The shop assistant, absorbed in her book, sold smoked fish and hollow bricks, hunting accessories, and hammocks in a room of less than two cubic meters. She didn't even look up when I entered and asked for a pair of seamless stockings; she just said (oh, how much I felt at home!) that *"без шва нет"* (*bez shva n'et*)—all sold out. Funny: just two months before, some boutique on the Rue de la Paix in Paris had made seamless stockings all the rage.

Wouldn't you know that the women living on the banks of the Angara River knew it.

26

What's Around the
Linguistic Corner?

≈

AGAIN, we have ended up on the subject of futurology; again, we should start it with a glance back.

According to the Old Testament, all humankind spoke a common language before Babel. The New Testament, when dealing with the first century A.D., mentions several languages, including those with such nice-sounding names as Pamphylian, Cappadocian, and Lycaonian.

Latin was dispersed to the far corners of the Roman Empire on the tips of soldiers' spears. Records show that the official written language was identical throughout the Empire. It is dazzling to imagine that the people of Lusitania, Mesopotamia, and Numidia were encouraged to pay the salt tax in the same words as the citizens of Pannonia[124] (who were perhaps not model taxpayers then, either).

When the fortunes of war reversed, this international language dissolved into the Romance languages: Italian, Spanish, Portuguese, French, Catalan, Provençal, Romansh, and Romanian. Of course, the local dialects first developed in speech and then crystallized into languages through writ-

---

124. A Roman province roughly corresponding to the western part of modern-day Hungary.

ten documents.

He who writes the history of languages chronicles humankind. A book like that, however, can present such a dry image of the exciting history of the lives and deaths of languages, just as a textbook on oceanography can fail to capture the mysterious world of the sea, or a cookbook the orgy of flavors within recipes.

The tide of languages spoken by people today flows over sunken Atlantises and submerged coral reefs. There is only one language that served general communication 2300 years ago as well as it does today: Hebrew. It must take its linguists no little trouble to find terms for new achievements of technology that comply with the rules of the language.

According to linguists, languages have both separated and conjoined throughout history. A high mountain or a river with a swift current once posed an obstacle to communication: two neighboring tribes would become separated and after a time could no longer understand one another. Today, however, I believe that the integration process is unstoppable. A voice can be received in a split second across an ocean. In the modern world, linguistic isolation is an anachronism.

English plays the role of Esperanto in science and technology. With its simple morphology and short words, it is very suitable for experts from around the world to use. Sometimes I wonder what a native speaker of English thinks when he hears two colleagues from, say, Norway and Croatia happily using highly technical (but broken) English that he can hardly understand. "What is the most widespread language in the world?" I am often asked. "Broken English," I tend to answer.

The spread of languages shouldn't imply the decay of national languages. There are so many literary and historical memories, so many joys and sorrows of the past linked to them that it is an obligation for all of us to guard their present and future.

Language is the reality of the life of a nation. At the end of 1945, the Japanese people, who had lost the war, became intensely self-critical. A Japanese journalist came up with the idea that Japanese should be discarded entirely and replaced with a European language like French. I was terrified. I felt like 100 million people were preparing for *hara-kiri*. He who knows other languages feels even closer to his own language. Goethe says in *Maximen und Reflexionen*: *"Wer fremde Sprachen nicht kennt, weiß nichts von seiner eigenen."* (Those who do not know foreign languages know nothing of their own.) Having used 16 languages, I feel about Hungarian as Kelemen Mikes[125] did about his hometown Zágon. In his still hardly rivaled masterpiece of Hungarian belles-lettres, Mikes writes: "I have come to like Rodosto so much that I cannot forget Zágon."

Fighters of the integration of languages were constructors of international languages. Several people have heard of Volapük, whose author, Johann Martin Schleyer, held that an international language should not have two features unpronounceable for most people: the sound /r/ and closed syllables (that is, those that end in a consonant). Both of these features pose insurmountable obstacles for the Chinese. On Beijing radio 40 years ago a tourist who had been to Moscow enthused about the beauty of *Kulinumulinu* for half an hour. I was about to become annoyed that I had missed such a tourist attraction when I realized he was talking about the Kremlin.[126] By the way, the word *Volapük* is coined from the words "world" and "speak," converted into a form that can be pronounced by most people regardless of their mother tongue.

---

125. Hungarian writer of the 18th century, a lifelong servant of the freedom-fighter Francis II Rákóczi. Born in Zágon (today: Zagon, Romania), he spent more than 40 years in Rodosto (today: Tekirdağ, eastern Turkey) serving his master-in-exile, despite never-ceasing homesickness.

126. The original Russian word Кремль (*Kreml*) is more difficult to pronounce with its two ending consonants.

In the first decades of the 20th century, there was such an abundance of proposed world languages that an international panel was called together to choose the most suitable one. Its members—with a representative of Hungary among them—found Esperanto, constructed by the Polish physician Zamenhof, the best, even if not perfect. It is still a widespread world language; it is more popular than Ido, which was developed on the advice of the above board, and Interlingua, promoted in the West.

Personally, I would happily select Esperanto, symbolized by a green star, as the hope of humankind. As a morphologist, however, I would find it difficult to familiarize myself with the unusual grammar forms (like adjectives ending with -*a* before nouns ending with -*o*). As an interpreter, I can only share the sentiment of the hypothetical physician who, when asked how he would feel if a miracle drug were invented, replied, "I would be happy because everybody wants to live. But I wouldn't mind if it were only released after my death, because I must live too."

Of course, it would be naiveté to think that with the acceptance of a common language, differences between people would cease. The reticent Englishman and the outgoing American speak practically the same language, but may be culturally far apart. And while that not all Italians are hot-blooded and not all Germans are meticulous, a certain national trait does exist. Language is one of its projections. Everyone who travels a lot experiences this. I would like to relate one such encounter—a kind one.

It happened in Mexico City, where I was interpreting at a conference. At lunchtime, I decided to do some sightseeing. As I roved the streets, I bumped into a romping crowd of children. They immediately joined me and came along with a vivid twittering. I would have enjoyed their shiny eyes and hearty laughs had a smudgy little palm not reached out and started to gesticulate in front of my nose, seeking a handout. I shrank away.

At a sort of marketplace, I saw a scale. Who can resist a thing like that, especially if one has been subjected to lots of protocol lunches and dinners? I stepped on it, but could not come up with the necessary coin—a 20 peso—in my purse: all I found were 10 peso coins. At that time what I feared happened. The smudgy little palm appeared in front of my nose with the desired copper coin shining in it. And when I was about to hand over its equivalent, its little owner bowed in front of me with a dignity suiting a proud hidalgo: *"¡Cortesía, Señora!"* (A gift, Madam!)

My casual acquaintances haven't only been street youngsters; there have been some crowned heads too. I would like to tell about one encounter here because I haven't had the opportunity to write about it yet.

A number of years ago I was in Tehran. Through some ploy, I managed to get an invitation to a reception of the then-ruler—Mohammed Reza Pahlavi, Shah of Iran. His majesty and his wife descended on me in person for a couple of words. They asked me what I had seen of their country and had some suggestions of what I should see. This royal favor moved me so much that when I arrived home, I wrote a fairly long article about it for a newspaper.

However, Iran had a revolution before the article could be published. The shah escaped and his reign was taken over by the Ayatollah Khomeini. Because of this, the article was rejected for being "out of date."

I am ashamed to admit that I was torn between my literary ambition and the truth. Why deny it: the former prevailed. I re-edited the article but this time with the Bearded One as the protagonist. By the time I had resubmitted it to the newspaper, however, he had proven to be no bed of roses either, and so it was rejected again. It is only now, two decades later and long after the manuscript has been lost, that this story occurs to me again.

Politics aside, my travels also taught me that people's

speech tends to be influenced not so much by their social affiliation as by the specific nature of their mother tongue.

Latin people tend to use superlatives. Anglo-Saxon people prefer understatement. If we ask a librarian whether we can stay a little longer when the library is near closing time and we get a mild "I'm afraid not," it is only in its literal meaning that it means a possible not; in practice it is equal to the flattest refusal.

Hungarian also has such understatements. "I would ask for a kilo of bread," we say in the bakery. Being definite is also a matter of manners—more exactly, bad manners—with the Japanese. One is supposed to say even one's plan for the current day as "I would like to go to Kyoto today, I would think so."

The English modal auxiliary verbs *shall–will* and *should–would* share some common ground in their usage. British English speakers hold that we can't use *will* after *I* or *we* in statements about the future; *shall* is the proper form. Regarding *should*, it is sometimes the past form of *shall* in unreal conditions (e.g., "If I were rich, I should buy..."). However, it can be replaced by *would*. And *shall* can be replaced by *should*, in most constructions.

No wonder that an American emigré of ours, Lajos Zilahy,[127] wrote: "My brain was eroded by *should–would*."

Until humankind matures to accept one or two international languages, the task of building bridges between languages is ahead of us, language students. When writing this book, I was guided by no other endeavor than to show that bridge-building doesn't necessarily have to consist of onerous brick-carrying: it can be a joyful manifestation of the proud human tradition to pursue and acquire knowledge.

---

127. Hungarian writer and playwright of the 20th century.

Epilogue

≈

I CANNOT thank those who patiently roamed with me in the realm of languages with more beautiful words than those of Cicero in "Pro Archia Poeta" (7.16):

> *...haec studia adulescentiam alunt, senectutem oblectant, res secundas ornant, adversis perfugium ac solacium praebent, delectant domi, non impediunt foris, pernoctant nobiscum, peregrinantur, rusticantur.*

> ...this study nurtures our youth, delights our old age, brightens the good times, and provides a refuge and comfort in bad times; literature brings us pleasure at home, does not hamper us at work, and is the companion of our nights, our travels, our country retreats.